what do we know and what should do about...?

inequality

Mike Brewer

Los Angeles | London | New Delhi
Singapore | Washington DC | Melbourne

Los Angeles | London | New Delhi
Singapore | Washington DC | Melbourne

SAGE Publications Ltd
1 Oliver's Yard
55 City Road
London EC1Y 1SP

SAGE Publications Inc.
2455 Teller Road
Thousand Oaks, California 91320

SAGE Publications India Pvt Ltd
B 1/I 1 Mohan Cooperative Industrial Area
Mathura Road
New Delhi 110 044

SAGE Publications Asia-Pacific Pte Ltd
3 Church Street
#10-04 Samsung Hub
Singapore 049483

Editor: Matthew Waters
Editorial assistant: Jasleen Kaur
Production editor: Katherine Haw
Copyeditor: Neville Hankins
Proofreader: Clare Weaver
Indexer: Charmian Parkin
Marketing manager: George Kimble
Cover design: Lisa Harper-Wells
Typeset by: C&M Digitals (P) Ltd, Chennai, India
Printed in the UK

Library of Congress Control Number: 2019937998

British Library Cataloguing in Publication data

A catalogue record for this book is available from the British Library

ISBN 978-1-5264-6040-0
ISBN 978-1-5264-6041-7 (pbk)

At SAGE we take sustainability seriously. Most of our products are printed in the UK using responsibly sourced papers and boards. When we print overseas we ensure sustainable papers are used as measured by the PREPS grading system. We undertake an annual audit to monitor our sustainability.

contents

titles in the series

about the series

Every news bulletin carries stories which relate in some way to the social sciences – most obviously politics, economics and sociology but also, often, anthropology, business studies, security studies, criminology, geography and many others.

Yet despite the existence of large numbers of academics who research these subjects, relatively little of their work is known to the general public. There are many reasons for that but one, arguably, is that the kinds of formats that social scientists publish in, and the way in which they write, are simply not accessible to the general public.

The guiding theme of this series is to provide a format and a way of writing which addresses this problem. Each book in the series is concerned with a topic of widespread public interest, and each is written in a way which is readily understandable to the general reader with no particular background knowledge.

The authors are academics with an established reputation and a track record of research in the relevant subject. They provide an overview of the research knowledge about the subject, whether this be long-established or reporting the most recent findings; widely accepted or still controversial. Often in public debate there is a demand for greater clarity about the facts, and that is one of the things the books in this series provide.

However, in social sciences, facts are often disputed and subject to different interpretations. They do not always, or even often, 'speak for themselves'. The authors therefore strive to show the different interpretations or the key controversies about their topics, but without getting bogged down in arcane academic arguments.

Not only can there be disputes about facts but also there are almost invariably different views on what should follow from these facts. And, in any case, public debate requires more of academics than just to report facts; it is also necessary to make suggestions and recommendations about the implications of these facts.

Thus each volume also contains ideas about 'what we should do' within each topic area. These are based upon the authors' knowledge of the field but also, inevitably, upon their own views, values and preferences. Readers may not agree with them, but the intention is to provoke thought and well-informed debate.

Chris Grey, Series Editor

Professor of Organization Studies

Royal Holloway, University of London

about the author

Mike Brewer is a Professor of Economics at the University of Essex and a Research Fellow at the Institute for Fiscal Studies. He studied Economics at the University of Cambridge and the University of Bristol, and has previously worked at HM Treasury. His research is on inequality, child poverty, and on how taxes and benefits affect household incomes and working patterns. He was a member of the National Equality Panel (2008–10), and has served on commissions or similar set up by the Joseph Rowntree Foundation, the Resolution Foundation and the Scottish Government. He was supported to write this by the ESRC through the Research Centre on Micro-Social Change (MiSoC) at the University of Essex, grant number ES/L009153/1, and declares that any royalties will be donated to charity. Learn more at **mikebrewereconomics.com/WDWK**

introduction

Inequality is bad and getting worse. (Angel Gurría, Secretary-General of the Organisation for Economic Co-operation and Development (OECD))[1]

Last year 26 people owned the same as the 3.8 billion people who make up the poorest half of humanity. (Oxfam)[2]

Top UK CEOs earn annual wage of average worker in 2½ days. (*Financial Times*, 4 January 2019)[3]

Reducing excessive inequality … is not just morally and politically correct, but it is good economics. (Christine Lagarde, Managing Director, International Monetary Fund)[4]

Never before have economic inequalities been so high up the news agenda. Not only campaigning organisations like Oxfam but also staid, sober, international organisations like the OECD say that inequality is too high. Inequality is said to be one of the reasons that the UK voted for Brexit, and the United States elected Donald Trump as President.[5] The economist Thomas Piketty toured the chat shows in 2014 with a book that analysed the causes of inequality; *The Economist* magazine in 2018 published a cartoon mocking the very rich (see Figure 1.1). And mainstream politicians in the United States are now advocating wealth taxes and new high rates of income tax.[6]

Concern is high now partly because economic inequality is at historically high levels. The OECD says that income inequality in developed countries is at its highest level for the past half century.[7] The combination

Figure 1.1

Source: Kevin KAL Kallaugher, *The Economist*, 29 November 2018, Kaltoons.com. Reproduced with permission

Note: 'Inbalance' in original.

of low growth and rising inequality has meant that, between 1980 and 2014, the richest 10% of adults in the United States captured 55% of the economic gains.[8] We also know more about how much inequality there is thanks to many researchers' hard work in uncovering and processing new sources of data. This has given us estimates from many countries over many years of the fraction of national income that goes to the very rich, and of how unequally distributed household wealth is.[9]

But there is also an increasing amount of academic research on the apparently harmful impacts of inequality. Unequal societies seem to be less healthy, less trusting, and tend to have more crime and violence. Many economists now recognise that a high level of inequality is not a natural, and certainly not a necessary, consequence of a vibrant economy; instead, key international organisations are worried that inequality is a drag on economic growth. We used to hope that, if there were some in society who had a lot less than others, then maybe this would be just a short-term blip, or that people could improve their lot with hard work and effort. We now know that a great deal of income mobility is short range and that, far from living in a world where all young people have equal chance to shine, where people end up in society is heavily influenced by where they started from. Indeed, there is a suggestion that high levels of inequality reduce social mobility, perpetuating divisions between families that have and those that have not (a society with lots of social mobility would be one where everyone has a similar chance of rising to the top, or falling to the bottom, or at least where that chance does not depend on their family background). And there is a fear – as set out by economists Joseph Stiglitz and Thomas Piketty – that these processes, combined with the way that economic inequalities affect our political debates, mean that the world will soon see economies with the sorts of gaps between the elites and the masses last seen in the early twentieth century. That would be profoundly undemocratic, and most definitely unfair.

In this book, I set out what is known about *economic inequalities* in the UK, or the differences in people's earnings, their disposable income and their wealth (I will define these precisely later), and I summarise what the academic literature says about the causes and consequences of high levels of inequality. Some might think that there is nothing wrong with some people being very well off, so long as their riches are deserved through hard work, effort or skill. My view is that inequality in the UK is too high, that too much of it represents inequalities in opportunities, and that we would all benefit if we could become a little more equal. That view is based on the evidence presented in this book – although not all of it is definitive, and these are ongoing areas of academic enquiry – but it also reflects my expert judgement after 21 years of implementing, studying or advising on social policy and social inequalities. With that in mind, I will also set out what could be done to move the UK off its high-inequality path.

Inequality in what?

What are economic inequalities?

This book will look at economic inequalities, that is the differences in people's earnings, their disposable income and their wealth. These three terms all have precise meanings and it will be good to be clear about them now.

Earnings – or pay, wages or salary – are what people in work are paid by their employer. For many people, earnings are their main, or only, source of income (across all people in the UK, 58% of our disposable income comes from earnings (after deducting taxes); see Figure 1.3 below).

In this book, I use the word *income* to refer to all the different sources of money that are coming into a household. As well as the earnings from employers, people can receive money from their own business or from being self-employed, or investment income from financial assets (such as interest on bank accounts, or dividend payouts on shares), or other sorts of income from other sorts of assets (buy-to-let investors get rental income, for example). Households may also receive money from the government in social security benefits or tax credits, such as the state pension or child benefit. Having received these different sources of income, most of us will have to pay taxes on some of that: what is left is *disposable income*. In Chapter 3, most of the discussion about income inequality refers to this concept of *disposable income*; the exception is when I look at the share of income going to the very rich, which measures income before deducting taxes.

My *wealth* is the value of all the physical belongings that I own (less any debts I owe), plus the value of any financial assets, like money in a bank account, shares or a pension fund. Income and wealth are two very different things. It is possible to have a high income but no wealth, and one can be very wealthy but have little income (like the tropes of the impoverished landowners of the early twentieth century, or elderly widows in large, impossible-to-heat houses). But income and wealth are usually related. If I have a low income, then that it is going to make it hard for me to generate much wealth of my own, and most forms of wealth do produce an income of some form, or can be sold and the money invested in assets that do produce income. And I will show in Chapter 3 that wealthy people in the UK tend also to have high incomes, and vice versa.

The distribution of income in the UK

The key facts on income inequality in the UK come from data collected by government statisticians. Every year, they ask tens of thousands of adults to tell them about their income (this is not easy: people usually do not like talking about their income, but if they ever call on you, please remember that my research depends on people sharing details of their lives with strangers).[10]

To turn the answers to these questions into a single number of 'income', statisticians decide over what period to measure income, whose income to measure, and what counts and does not count as income. There are several points about the definition used that you need to know (for more detail, see **mikebrewereconomics.com/WDWK**). First, the measure of income misses out on many things which can be important in determining your overall standard of living, such as what you are able to do when you are not at work, how much you benefit from free public services, and whether you own your own house (government statisticians do use another measure of income – known as 'income after housing costs' – where what is spent on housing is deducted from income, but this does not accurately reflect the savings that people can make if they own their own house, and in this book I always use the conventional 'before housing costs' measure). Second, we add up all the income of people living in the same household; this means that we cannot look at inequalities between (say) men and women in the same household. Third, income is measured over a short period of time – the last few weeks, more or less – and expressed in a weekly amount (alternatives would be to measure annual income, or even income over a lifetime). Finally, we measure income at a point in time. In general, I am less concerned about income inequality if individuals are moving about the income distribution from year to year, so that those who are well off now are likely to be poor later on. However, we know that, although incomes do change, the vast majority of moves are short-distance.[11]

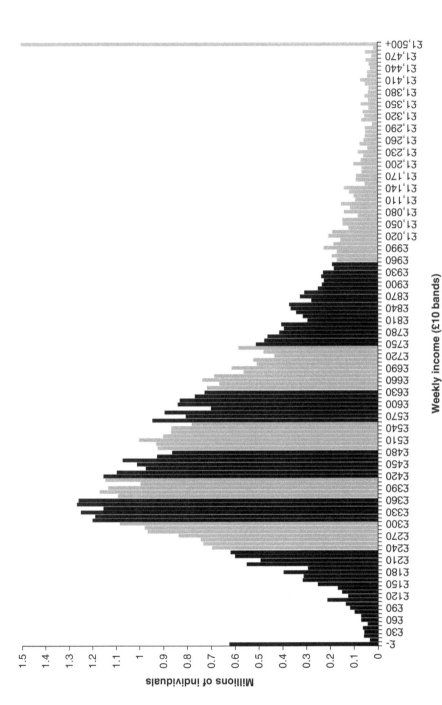

Figure 1.2 The distribution of income in the UK, 2016–17

Source: Based on data underpinning Figure 2.1 in Cribb et al. (2018)

Figure 1.2 shows the income distribution in the UK in 2016–17 (data for 2017–18 was released in March 2019, too late to be fully incorporated in this book).[12] Each bar represents a band of income £10 a week wide, and the height of the bar shows how many people have that much income. Here, 'income' has been added up across all members of a household and adjusted by the number of adults and children living in the household.[13] A lot of people are clumped together towards the bottom of the income distribution – around £300 to £400 a week – and a few people have high incomes that stretch out towards the right. At the very right of the figure, you can see the people whose income goes 'off the scale': there are more than 1.5 million in this bar, or about 2% of the population. It also seems to be the case that there are 600,000 people with no income at all. This would be alarming if true, but the consensus is that many of these do really have some income but have not reported it to the survey.[14] The mathematical average income in 2016–17 – that is, 'average' in the sense of 'add up everyone's income and share it out equally' – was £594 a week, considerably higher than the median income of £494. The fact that these are different reflects that some people in the UK have very high incomes. The figure also marks with alternate black and white shading what are called *the decile groups*: each of these groups contains 10% of the population.

It is also helpful to understand the different ways in which households in different parts of the income distribution get their income. Figure 1.3 shows what fraction of income comes from the four main sources, calculated separately for each decile group of the income distribution. Overall, 58% of household disposable income comes from (after tax) earnings from employment (as an employee of a company or charity or public sector body), 17% from social security benefits and tax credits, 11% savings, investments and people's private pension (payments of the basic state pension are counted in 'social security benefits or tax credits'), and 10% is income (after tax) from self-employment earnings or profits. Earnings become more important as a source of income as we move up the income distribution from poorest to richest (other than the very top, where there is a lot of income from self-employment), as does income from savings (although there is also a lot of income from savings at the very bottom of the income distribution). Income from social security benefits becomes more important as we move down the income distribution.

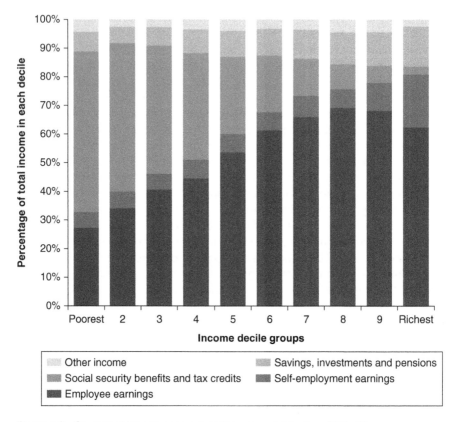

Figure 1.3 Sources of income across the UK income distribution, 2016–17

Source: Based on analysis provided by the Institute for Fiscal Studies of 'Households Below Average Income' data

Inequality of outcomes or inequality of opportunity?

There is an argument that we do not need to care about inequalities in *outcomes*, like income or wealth, provided that we live in a world where everyone has an equal *opportunity* to be rich or poor.[15] The idea is that our economic outcomes reflect the choices that we make, and it is right for us to face the consequences of those choices. But outcomes are also shaped by opportunities, and the extent of our opportunities are limited (or expanded) by our family, our employers, institutions, the current state of the economy, and so on, and are ever-changing. In a society where we cared only about equality of opportunities, would we give extra assistance to those who developed a longstanding illness? What about to someone whose employer went bankrupt because of competition from China? Or because of a fraudulent finance director? Would we help those whose opportunities are reduced because they are caring for children, or elderly parents, or whose marriage has broken down? In practice, identifying which unequal outcomes reflect unequal opportunities and which different choices is almost impossible. We can also argue that our opportunities to thrive as a citizen or to exercise our rights are inevitably constrained by our economic resources. More worryingly, it seems that the more unequal outcomes are now, the more unequal opportunities will become in the future, thanks to how parents strive for the best for their children, and how our democracies and politics seem to work (I discuss this more in the next chapter). Equality of outcomes is an excellent goal to strive for – and some of the suggested policy changes in Chapter 5 will help us move towards that – but we also need to care about inequality in outcomes.

Inequality or poverty?

There is also an argument made that we should be focused on relieving or alleviating poverty in the UK, and that we do not need to care about overall inequality. This seemed to be the view of Tony Blair, Prime Minister from 1997 to 2007, who said that 'I don't care if there are people who earn a lot of money. They are not my concern. I do care about people who are without opportunity, disadvantaged and poor.'[16] Of course, this does not have to be an either–or situation: it is possible to think that high rates of poverty and high levels of inequality are both problems we should try to tackle. The arguments that I will present later suggest that inequality is harmful to society over and above the harm that can be caused by living in poverty. They are separate problems, and an anti-poverty strategy would look different from an anti-inequality strategy even if policy makers happily accept that poverty, like inequality, is a relative concept. But there are strong links: reducing inequality in economic resources and increasing equality of opportunities will make reducing poverty a little easier.

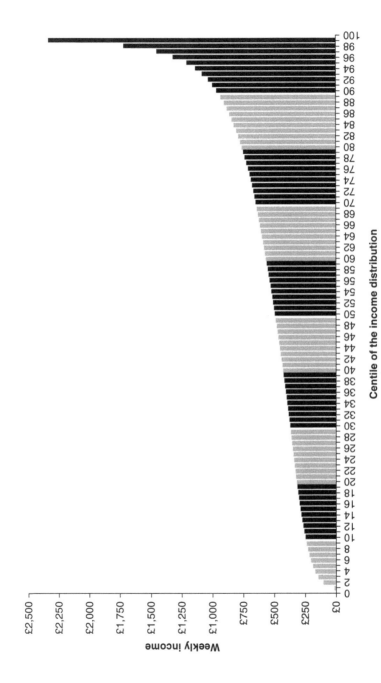

Figure 1.4 A Pen's Parade for the UK income distribution, 2016–17

Source: Data provided by the Institute for Fiscal Studies, derived from the 'Households Below Average Income' data-set

How can we visualise or measure inequality?

When thinking about income inequality, Jan Pen, a Dutch economist working in the 1970s, imagined a parade of people walking, with the poorest at the front and the richest at the back, and their height being proportional to their income, so that the person on average income was the height of an average person. This parade would start with some very short people. After half the people had walked past, we still would not have reached an averagely tall person; some time later, the parade would end with some giants.

Rather than watching actual people parade, we can draw this on a graph, with the height of each bar representing someone's income. In a perfectly equal society, everyone would have the same income, and the bars would all have the same height. In all real societies, the graph will have bars that get taller and taller as we move to the right.

Figure 1.4 shows Pen's Parade for the distribution of household income in the UK in 2016–17, but having left out the richest 1% of individuals (over 0.6m people), and having labelled the horizontal axis according to people's rank in the distribution of income, with the poorest person scoring 0 and the richest person scoring 100, and so on (these are called centiles or percentiles).

This figure also splits the population into 10 equal-sized decile groups. The boundary between the bottom (poorest) and second bottom of these decile groups is the 10th centile of the income distribution: a person at this point in the income distribution is richer than 1 in 10 of the population, but poorer than 9 out of 10. At the other end, someone at the boundary of the top (richest) and next-to-top decile group is at the 90th centile, and they are richer than 90% of the population but poorer than 10%. Reading off the vertical axis, you can see that a person at the 10th centile of the income distribution (on about £250 a week in 2016–17) has about half as much income as Mr or Mrs Average at the 50th centile – the middle of the distribution (on about £494 a week). And Mr or Mrs Average have slightly more than half as much income as someone at the 90th centile (on £962 a week) – that is, someone who is just outside the richest 10% of the population. These figures give us one commonly used measure of inequality, *the 90:10 ratio*. This is the income of the person at the 90th centile divided by the income of the person at the 10th centile, and the higher the number, the more inequality there is. For the UK in 2016–17, this was 3.9 for income (it was 6.3 for the United States, which tends to be top of the inequality league table, and 3.3 for Sweden, which tends to be a very equal country). The 90:10 ratio is easy to explain, and has a practical advantage that it does not use the data on incomes from the very top or bottom of the distribution that are often measured less accurately, or with more uncertainty, than more normal incomes. But its simplicity means that it is a broad-brush measure: a hypothetical inequality-reducing policy that took money from people at the 80th centile and gave it to people at the 20th centile would not change the 90:10 ratio.

Where are the top 1%?

I left the richest 1% out of Figure 1.4 so as to stop the scale on the vertical axis from shooting off the page. The 99th centile of weekly disposable income in 2016–17 was £2,317, which is more than twice (it is actually 2.4 times) the income of the 90th centile, but there were about another 660,000 adults and children in households with incomes above that. I will come back to the experiences of the very rich several times in this book, because of the way they affect measures of inequality, and their influence on the economy and society (and I will also show that the value of the 99th centile quoted above is probably an underestimate of the truth).

Income shares and Lorenz curves

Pen's Parade lets us visualise inequality, but does not measure it. A useful way to compare income distributions is to think about 'income shares', and then to plot these in a variant to Pen's Parade where people are lined up from the poorest to the richest, and we plot *the share of total income that goes to them plus all the people on their left* (i.e. who have less income than they do). In an economy where everyone has the same income, the poorest 1% in society will collectively have a total income of exactly 1% of the economy-wide total. But in the UK, the poorest 1% of people, all of whom had less than £16 a week income in 2016–17, are collectively going to have a share of the total UK-wide income that is a lot less than 1%, and the richest 1%, all of whom had at least £2,317 a week in 2016–17, will collectively have a lot more than 1% of the economy-wide income.

In Figure 1.5, I plot these income shares for each centile in the UK income distribution. This produces a curve that starts at zero, initially rises

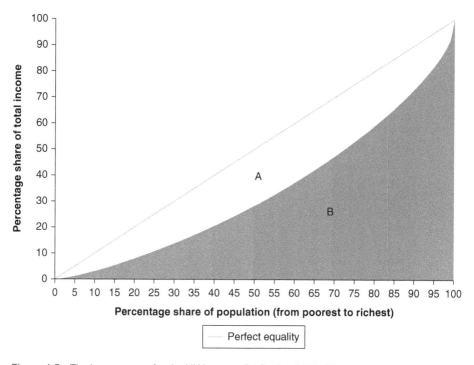

Figure 1.5 The Lorenz curve for the UK income distribution 2016–17

Source: Based on analysis provided by the Institute for Fiscal Studies of 'Households Below Average Income' data

slowly, but then rises more and more quickly until it reaches 100%. It is called a Lorenz curve, and you can use it to read off income shares. If you start from a point on the horizontal axis, go up until you hit the curve, and then read across to the vertical axis, you can read what fraction of total income goes to the poorest section of the population. In the UK in 2016–17, the poorer 50% got just over 28% of total household income. Or you can start on the vertical axis and read the graph the other way, so you would see (for example) that half of total household income went to (coincidentally) the richest 28% of the UK.

The Lorenz curve is the idea behind one of the most commonly used measures of inequality: the Gini coefficient (or index). The Gini coefficient measures how close the Lorenz curve (as plotted in Figure 1.5) is to being a straight line (which would correspond to our perfectly equal society). Mathematically, it is the area A divided by the total of area A and area B. The more inequality there is, the 'curvier' the Lorenz curve will be (i.e. it will start off close to the horizontal axis before rising rapidly to reach 100%). If everyone had the same income the Gini coefficient would be zero as there would be no inequality. If a single person had all the money in the economy and the rest had nothing, then the Gini would be 1. For the UK in 2016–17, the Gini coefficient was 0.337.

The ratio of areas on a graph is a rather abstract measure of inequality. But it turns out that if two random British people bumped into each other, and you then subtracted the poorer person's income from the richer person's income, and expressed that as a ratio of the average income in the country, then on average you would expect to get a difference of exactly twice the Gini coefficient. (In other words, the difference in incomes between two random Brits would on average be about 2 × 0.337, or 67%, of the national average income, or just under £21,000 a year in 2016–17 in equivalent-£-per-couple-with-no-children. That number will appear to some to be too high. Surely, you might say, if I think of all the people I know, it cannot be the case that the average difference between my income and theirs is £21,000? In reality, that difference probably would be a lot smaller than £21,000 because all the people you know are not a random selection of people from across the income distribution.)

A really important point: most measures of inequality are about living standards relative to other people

When economists talk about inequality, they say that it is a *relative* concept. What they mean is that the amount of inequality depends on how high my income is *relative to other people's*. Imagine the UK redefined its own currency overnight, so instead of using sterling, we used Brewers, where 1 Brewer is valued at £100. This is just a change of labels, and clearly this should have no real impact on our society. Luckily, then, changing from pounds to Brewers will not change any of the measures of inequality that we use: the amount of inequality in a country does not depend on the units used to measure income. That is very sensible.

Now imagine coming back to the UK, still happily measuring income in Brewers, in 20 years' time. There has been some economic growth, and by a huge coincidence every individual's income is exactly twice what it was 20 years ago. If this happened, then most measures of inequality *still would not have changed*. If this seems wrong – perhaps you think that a situation where everyone's income doubles actually makes things worse, because the gap (in pounds or Brewers) between the richest and the poorest is even more insurmountable – then you will need to find other statistics to monitor alongside the traditional, relative measures of inequality that I use in this book.

Economic inequalities in the UK in one chart

Figure 1.6 shows trends over time in the Gini coefficients of individual hourly pay, disposable income and household wealth as well as share of income going to the top 1%.

The key points are that:

- income inequality in the UK was low in the 1960s to early 1980s. It rose rapidly through the 1980s, and has remained at its new higher level ever since (although I will modify this story slightly in Chapter 3 when I focus on what has happened to the super-rich in the UK);

- the fraction of pre-tax income going to the richest 1% of adults rose steadily from the late 1970s to the late 2000s. It fell back after the financial crisis in 2008, but it is rising again and is close to a record high, at just under 15% of income;

- inequality in hourly rates of pay rose throughout the 1980s and 1990s, peaked in the early 2000s, and has fallen since;

- wealth is a lot more unequally distributed than hourly pay or disposable income and, as will be shown in Chapter 3, household wealth in the UK has been growing in importance since the 1970s, driven more by rises in house prices than by active saving.

That rise in income inequality in the 1980s (about 10 percentage points in 15 years) was one of the largest increases seen across developed nations' economies. Figure 1.7 shows that the UK is now close to the top of the international league table for inequality. The UK has the second

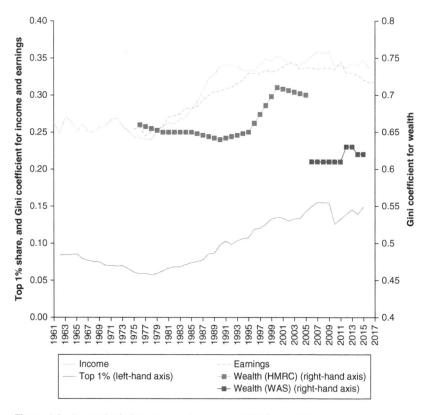

Figure 1.6 Inequality in income, earnings and wealth in the UK

Sources: Income: Figure 3.7 of Cribb et al. (2018), derived from the 'Households Below Average Income' data-set. Earnings: from Box 2 of D'Arcy (2018). Wealth: Table 2.5 of ONS (2018a), Table 2.3 of Hills et al. (2013)

highest level of inequality among the countries with the seven largest economies (the G7), behind the United States. Elsewhere in Europe, only Lithuania is more unequal. Among the countries highlighted in Figure 1.7 (which include the 36 members of the OECD, which tend to be the richest countries, as well as some newly industrialised countries), those that are more unequal than the UK include China, Brazil, India, Mexico and South Africa.

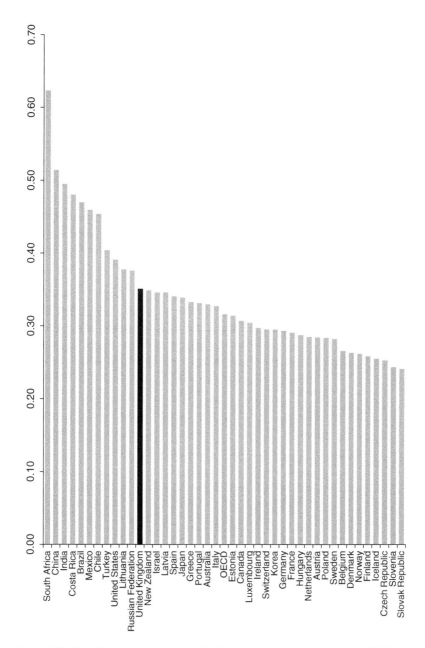

Figure 1.7 The Gini coefficient across OECD and selected other countries, 2016 or latest year

Source: www.oecd.org/social/soc/IDD-Key-Indicators.xlsx

Researchers also measure income inequality across the world: global inequality, although very high (with a Gini of over 0.7), seems to be falling at the moment. This is because the incomes of many people in some large, developing countries are rising at a faster rate than those in developed countries. On the other hand, the global elite are doing very well, and are seeing some of the highest income growth.[17]

Growing inequality is a problem in many developed countries: if the UK could return to the level of inequality it had in the mid-1970s (a Gini of around 0.25), it would find itself as one of the most equal countries in 2016. The fact that income inequality varies so much between countries that are at similar levels of economic development, and that it changed by so much in such a short space of time in the UK in the 1980s, are important clues that the high levels of inequality seen now in the UK are not inevitable.

It is also worth thinking about how much income inequality there would be if people did not have to not pay income tax or national insurance payments, or if people did not receive social security benefits like child benefit, universal credit or the state pension. Unsurprisingly, the gap between the rich and poor would be greater if there were no taxes on income. It would not be much larger, though: the Gini would go up by about 0.03 (remember, it was 0.337 in 2016–17). Social security benefits and tax credits do a lot more to keep inequality down: without them, the Gini would be another 0.11 higher.[18]

The rest of this book

In Chapter 2, I will set out some of the research from the past two decades on the impact of inequality. It is clear that countries with high levels of inequality have worse health outcomes and greater social problems than more equal societies, and I will discuss the arguments – made by, among others, Richard Wilkinson and Kate Pickett – that these problems are worse *because of* high levels of inequality. I will set out the evidence that inequality hurts economic performance, and may even have caused the financial crash of 2008 and the subsequent Great Recession. I will show how high levels of inequality seem to make it impossible to have equality of opportunity, because of what parents do to give their children the best chance in life, as summarised very recently by Matthias Doepke and Fabrizio Zilibotti. And I will summarise the landmark work of Thomas Piketty, who argued that, left unchecked, the way that wealth accumulates and is bequeathed from generation to generation risks leading to ever-growing inequalities and the emergence of a super-wealthy elite.

In Chapter 3, 'What do we know about inequality?', I present the key trends in economic inequality in the UK. I will explain how the UK became so much more unequal during the 1980s, why inequality stopped rising in the 1990s, and how it has been changing since the financial crash in 2008. Given the importance of the very rich in the key theories of why inequality can be harmful, I will zoom in to see what is known about the top 1% in the UK – the 536,000 people with the highest incomes – as well as the top 0.1% and top 0.01%. And I will show that the widely held view that inequality in the UK is not getting worse is based on statistics that conceal a sharp rise in the share of income going to those with the highest incomes, and actually may not be true.[19] I will also look at what we know about the distribution of wealth, where new, better sources of household data show that ownership of wealth is far more widespread than it was a century ago. But there remain enormous differences between those who have little or no (or even negative) wealth and those with, for example, homes that have more than doubled in value in the last 30 years (in real terms) or generous pension pots. And I will assess the relevance to the UK of Thomas Piketty's prediction that growing wealth inequalities and inheritances are set to return our economies to levels of inequality last seen at the dawn of the twentieth century.

Chapter 4 addresses the challenge of 'What should we do about inequality?'. My calls for action fall into six areas: towards a fairer labour market; curbing excessive pay at the top; redistributing wealth; providing security and opportunity for all; promoting social mobility; and publishing better analysis about the state of economic inequalities in the UK. Some of the policy responses respond to the facts about economic inequalities as set out in Chapter 3, or attempt to address the causes; others respond to the way that inequalities harm our society, as set out in Chapter 2. Some of these will seem radical, or politically unfeasible. But if those in power want a different outcome, then we can choose different paths, and who can say how politically feasible it will be to have ever-growing divides in society? Finally, a section at the end suggests further reading and gives details of the key data sources and **mikebrewereconomics.com/WDWK** looks at some of the detailed issues involved in measuring incomes and inequality.

There is much that is missing from a short book like this. There is no space to talk about geographical inequalities in the UK, but it is worrying that they remain stubbornly persistent.[20] There is a new concern in the UK about differences between generations or cohorts, driven by the undeniable fact that the old idea that each generation will be better off than its predecessors has broken down for Millennials (those born after 1980).[21] I will not look at income mobility, or about incomes over the lifetime.[22] I will not talk about other forms of inequality, such as in health, nor about differences between different groups in society – such as between men and women (think of the gender pay gap) – or differences in, say, wealth between those of different ethnic backgrounds. I will not talk about social class, even though, in the UK at least, class is part of the reason why inequalities persist across generations.[23] And I will not look at the link between inequality and politics. The focus of this book is on the UK, but I will show how the UK compares with other developed countries.

background

The 'politics of envy' is a phrase used to pour scorn on those seeking greater equality. The accusation is that those wanting more equality are envious: they simply cannot tolerate that other people have become more successful, and they want some of that wealth for themselves. But one reason that curbing inequality is now recognised as a global priority is the recent build-up of evidence that shows, or claims to show, that high levels of inequality are actively harmful.

The research falls into two areas, with researchers arguing that:

1. high levels of inequality make us less healthy and die younger, be more violent and less trusting, be more anxious and less happy;

2. high levels of inequality hurt economic performance, and greatly exacerbated – and possibly even caused – the financial crash of 2008 and the subsequent Great Recession.

Meanwhile, other researchers have been arguing that inequalities perpetuate from one generation to the next. Researchers have presented evidence to argue that:

1. high levels of inequality reduce social mobility, or make it impossible to have equality of opportunity, because of what parents do to give their children the best chance in life;

2. the way that wealth accumulates and is bequeathed from generation to generation risks leading to ever-growing inequalities and the emergence of a super-wealthy elite.

These are bold claims, and it is hard to prove convincingly that there is a cause and effect relationship for all of these phenomena. Research, rightly, continues, but there is no doubt that these new studies have changed the public narrative on inequality, and altered policy in key institutions.

Claim: inequality makes us more stressed and less healthy, less trusting and more violent

Richard Wilkinson and Kate Pickett were among the first to assemble a comprehensive charge sheet against income inequality. Their first book, *The Spirit Level* (2009), reviewed hundreds of papers and presented new research that show how people in more unequal societies tend to be more obese, less healthy, die younger, be more stressed and have more mental health problems, take more drugs, be less trusting and be more violent, and have children who do less well in school. Their work had a powerful impact on public debate in the UK, and was praised by politicians from both the Conservative and the Labour Parties.[24] Figure 2.1 shows their summary of this relationship, with the level of income inequality being higher in countries with more social and health problems. It is not the case that these problems go away as countries get richer, and what we see is not caused solely by the fact that the most vulnerable end up at the bottom of society and experience these problems more than others. Instead, Wilkinson and Pickett argued that high levels of inequality make these social problems worse, and do so right across society.

This work attracted a great deal of comment and attention. Much of the analysis presented in *The Spirit Level* was based on relatively simple statistical analysis comparing unequal countries with equal countries. This is not a reliable way to establish a cause and effect relationship. Wilkinson and Pickett know this, of course, and the explanations they put forward are based on the results of hundreds of peer-reviewed papers; the graphical relationships shown in their book were just a powerful way to make a point. On the other hand, not all of the arguments in the book have solid underpinnings in research. The most reliable studies that look at whether

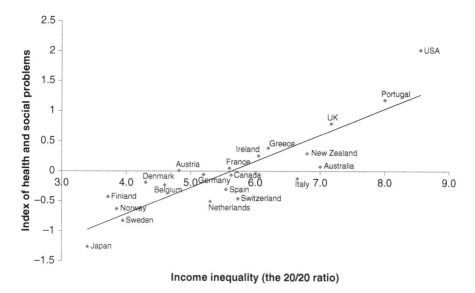

Figure 2.1 Income inequality is correlated with social problems across countries

Source: Based on data made available by The Equality Trust and shown in Figure 2.2 in Wilkinson and Pickett (2009)

income inequality affects health often find no effects, or very small effects.[25] And the idea that income inequality makes some of these outcomes worse *for everyone* in society has not yet been established conclusively (we do know that, for example, people in Sweden have better health than people in the UK, who in turn have better health than people in the United States, across all parts of society, but we do not know whether that is due to the lower level of inequality).

But Wilkinson and Pickett argue that there are many reasons to think that inequality is the true cause. First, there is the sheer weight and robustness of the evidence. It is not just a comparison of the United States against Sweden (say): Wilkinson and Pickett found that various outcomes were related to inequality when comparing different countries, but they also looked within the United States and found that unequal states are less happy, less healthy, more violent, and so on, than more equal states. Wilkinson and Pickett argue that the idea that something else is making these social problems worse, and that in turn leads to greater inequality ('reverse causality'), seems unlikely, because that would not explain why countries that do bad in one of these social outcomes (such as high rates of obesity) also do bad in others (such as violence and use of drugs). There could always be a hidden factor causing both inequality and social problems, but Wilkinson and Pickett say that many researchers have tried and failed to identify what this might be. Finally, for many of the outcomes in *The Spirit Level*, there are plausible theories why inequality has harmful effects (in the jargon, these are called 'pathways'). In some instances, it is possible to focus on part of a possible pathway and see that there is a true cause and effect relationship. But we cannot roll back time and see what would happen to crime, or health, or trust, if Sweden (say) were to have experienced US-style levels of inequality. And it can be difficult to disprove the counter-claim that, say, the United States has (much) more crime than Sweden because of something unique about the United States or Sweden, and not because of inequality at all. So research continues.

'All the people like us are We, and everyone else is They'[26]

In their second book, *The Inner Level* (2018), Wilkinson and Pickett set out a clearer, unified explanation for why they think inequality leads to these problem outcomes. They say that 'the more hierarchical is society, the stronger the idea that people are ranked according to inherent differences in worth or value, and the greater their insecurities about self-worth'. High levels of inequality, they argue, heighten anxieties (or stress) over our social status; these in turn worsen aspects of consumerism ('keeping up with the Joneses'), lead to feelings of entitlement for those at the top and shame for those at the bottom, and reduce social mixing, trust and social cohesion. Michael Marmot had argued in 2004 that those on low incomes tend to have less autonomy or control over their lives, and fewer opportunities for social engagement and participation, and that these lead to social inequalities in health.[27] We know that anxieties about status can lead to stress, and then ill-health, and the idea of so-called 'social anxiety' has been explored in the popular press by authors including Alain de Botton in 2005. And the idea that having a low income can lead to feelings of shame is discussed by Thorstein Veblen at the end of the nineteenth century, and Adam Smith in the eighteenth century. The additional steps in the argument made by Wilkinson and Pickett are that high levels of income inequality make social anxieties and the shame of poverty worse, and that anxieties about social status can explain a wide set of social problems.

These claims are not accepted by all, but it seems likely that they are part of the reason why inequality goes hand-in-hand with more social problems, and so it is worth exploring them a little more. Wilkinson and Pickett's argument starts with the idea that, as income gaps grow, there is an ever-increasing cachet to being rich and it becomes more shameful to be poor; money, and what one does with it, become evermore important to our social status. As a result these high levels of inequalities drive us to do things that increase our status or protect ourselves against an encroachment from the less worthy. Here, there are strong echoes of the phenomenon observed by Thorstein Veblen in the nineteenth century. Veblen wrote about how any self-respecting gentleman of leisure can be seen buying things 'beyond the minimum required for subsistence and physical efficiency'. But then, he argued:

> [s]ince the consumption of these more excellent goods is an evidence of wealth, it becomes honorific; and conversely, the failure to consume in due quantity and quality becomes a mark of inferiority and demerit. (Veblen, 1899)

Veblen used the term 'conspicuous consumption' to refer to a situation where one is spending more on goods and services not because of some direct benefit of owning them or using them, but because of what is conveyed by the act of owning that good or using the service. Does a Swiss watch tell the time so much better than one from China? Is flying first class really 10 times nicer than flying standard? Almost certainly not: the reason that people spend in ways like this is bound up in feelings to do with the social status that comes from owning such goods or using such services. The situation Veblen describes might at first seem harmless: like the Emperor's new clothes, does it matter if the rich have frivolous, expensive habits? Well, it wouldn't if their spending habits did not affect the rest of us. But we demonstrate social status with the stuff that we can afford to consume, and such is the status that comes from being rich that the lifestyles led by the very rich themselves become desirable.

You might just think that this is a damning indictment on our culture of worshipping celebrities and Instagramming our lives to death ('I am not allowed to earn lots of money because it might make you sad?!', a sceptical plutocrat might wonder). But this response reflects how our brains are wired. We are social creatures, Wilkinson and Pickett argue, and social status is important to our sense of self-esteem, and threats to our social status lead to feelings of insecurity and undermine our self-confidence. Veblen observed these desires to establish superiority (among the rich), and the need to conform (among the slightly less rich), in the nineteenth-century United States: it is nothing to do with our selfie-obsessed, digital age. And advertisers have for decades exploited our anxieties about status because they know it works.[28] It may be that these processes and reactions are so ingrained into our modern consumerist world that we cannot imagine a world without them.

Other implications of this heightened awareness of differences that comes in highly unequal societies, and the extra importance that is placed on money or status, are an inflated sense of pride or narcissism among those at the top of the pile – a strong belief that their position is due to their own talents and effort[29] – and a sense of shame or resentment at the lack of status at the bottom. Feelings of shame or pride in turn reduce feelings of trust and empathy, and reduce social cohesion, something that is clearly shown by cross-national comparisons of trust or civic participation, which tend to be higher in more equal societies. As Tony Atkinson describes, '[t]he post-1980 rise in income inequality has reinforced the opposition to redistribution and has strengthened support for economic policies, such as market liberalisation, that contribute to inequality: a cumulative process is in operation'.[30] At the extreme, violence and many forms of anti-social behaviour can be in part seen as a way of ensuring status or a response to losing it.

Claim: inequality hurts economic performance

A stereotypical view of economists is that they are focused on making our economy as productive as possible – the metaphor deployed at this point is usually 'maximising the size of the pie' – and that they leave politicians or philosophers to worry about inequality – or how the pie is divided. Our stereotypical economists, indeed, would probably think that high levels of inequality are signs of a vibrant economy, and that any attempt to resist an unequal distribution of pie will lead to less pie for all. But there is an emerging view that high levels of inequalities might be bad for economic performance: the more pie goes to the very rich (the very greedy?), the smaller the pies will be in the future.

The earliest work in this area looked at how economic growth might affect inequality. Simon Kuznets, a Nobel-Prize-winning economist working in the 1950s, argued that it would be normal for countries to become first more and then less unequal as they progressed from a mostly agricultural economy (think of Britain in the late seventeenth century) to one dominated by industry and services. But the new research approaches the problem in the opposite direction, asking how inequality affects economic growth. This analysis is based on looking across countries (or regions within countries) over long periods of time, and seeing what happens to growth after spells of especially high or low inequality. This is statistically challenging, and it has proven hard to assess how strong – and even in what direction – the link is between inequality and economic performance, just as it is hard to learn about the links between inequality and the social outcomes that Wilkinson and Pickett were concerned with. Again, research is continuing, and it would be wrong to say that there is an academic consensus.

But both the Organisation for Economic Co-operation and Development (the OECD) and the International Monetary Fund (the IMF; definitely not known for being left-of-centre or social democratic) now conclude that, on average, high levels of inequality in a country lead to periods of lower, and less stable, economic growth in the future, and raise the risk of economic and political crises; this work is summarised in the 2019 book by Jonathan Ostry and co-authors.[31] The most recent studies have investigated how the links between inequality and growth might vary across countries. One study suggested that the negative impact of inequality on growth is especially large in the Western hemisphere countries (dominated by South America), considerably smaller in European countries, and almost zero across all developed countries, on average; another found that higher inequality was bad for economic growth except in the poorest countries, where it stimulated growth.[32] The IMF estimates that a 1 percentage point fall in the Gini coefficient in the UK could permanently increase growth rates by just under 0.1 percentage points.[33] Similarly, OECD research implies that the UK economy could have grown 20% faster over the 1990–2010 period had inequality remained at its 1985 level, which would mean our economy would now be 6% larger than it is now (although the OECD study probably overstates the negative impact of inequality on growth).[34]

So why does inequality reduce economic growth? Many of the theories that I just looked at – that high levels of inequality make us unwell, less trusting, more selfish, and so on – will also directly weaken the performance of our economy. Another idea is that a more unequal society is more sensitive to the economic cycle (and there is a vicious circle here: economic instability, in general, will worsen inequality, because the rich are much more likely to have resources which they can fall back on in tough times, which leads to greater instability in future). But there is also a link from economic inequality to politics and policy, and one of the mechanisms is that increased inequality might lead to political instability or a lack of social consensus – the feeling that 'we are all in it together'. This in turn might mean that countries spend less on universal public services, or invest less in physical infrastructure or in their citizens' education and skills than they otherwise would, or be less likely to take difficult decisions when hit by crises. All of these could lower future economic growth.[35]

Joseph Stiglitz, a former Chief Economist of the World Bank and a winner of the Nobel Prize in Economics, has become a very vocal critic of inequality, and is especially critical of the harmful influence of the very rich on economic, political and cultural life in the United States.[36] In his 2012 book, he argued that apparent success of the very rich reflects a great deal of what economists call 'rent-seeking'. What he means is that large remunerations at the top are not a reward for hard work, effort, talent or ideas, but reflect gains made at other people's expense, thanks to failures in the economy, or in the government's ability to regulate. His examples of rent-seeking include companies exploiting scarce natural resources, overcharging government agencies, profiting from markets where they have near-monopolies, or taking advantage of differences in the information available to the buyer and the seller (most of the financial sector, he argues). If he is right, then high inequalities are a *symptom* of an inefficient economy: if we could make these markets work more effectively, then the economy would perform better *and* we would have more equality. But once high levels of inequalities exist, Stiglitz argues, those who are benefitting from market failures find it more worthwhile to protect their exploitative positions than they do to innovate or generate value for the rest of society. If he is right, then high inequalities are a *cause* of an inefficient economy in the future. As the OECD says:

The notion that one can enjoy the benefits from one's own efforts has always been a powerful incentive to invest in human capital, new ideas and new products, as well as to undertake risky commercial ventures. But beyond a certain point, and not least during an economic crisis, growing income inequalities can undermine the foundations of market economies. They can eventually lead to inequalities of opportunity. This smothers social mobility, and weakens incentives to invest in knowledge. The result is a misallocation of skills, and even waste through more unemployment, ultimately undermining efficiency and growth potential. (www.oecd.org/economy/growth-and-inequality-close-relationship.htm)

The high levels of inequality in the United States and elsewhere are certainly implicated in the financial crisis of 2008.[37] The immediate cause was failures in the market for mortgages in the US. We can debate how much blame lies with the people that applied for mortgages, the bankers that lent money, the institutions supposedly regulating them, or the politicians that empowered the regulators, but, at its nub, too many mortgages were being lent to people who could not afford them, and against properties whose value was inflated through a housing boom. Many argue that that the weak growth in income through much of the 1990s and 2000s in the United States, in combination with the racing away of incomes at the top, meant that people were keen to borrow more to stop their standard of living from falling behind (this is 'keeping up with the Joneses' again). At the same time, the fact that so much of the gains from economic growth were being captured by the very rich was slowing the economy down, because the very rich tend to save more of their income than the rest of society. As a result, central banks kept interest rates low to stimulate the economy; but by doing so, they created cheap credit and an unsustainable house price bubble.[38]

So, some mainstream economists now believe that too much inequality is harmful to a country's economic performance. What is more surprising is that work by the IMF and OECD has found no strong evidence that policy interventions that governments take to reduce inequality have any detrimental impacts on growth (except in the most extreme cases).[39] This is a controversial finding, given that classical – or, better, 'stylised' – economic thinking would suggest that anything governments can do to fix inequalities will hurt the economy. If the IMF is right, then we need to stop thinking about a trade-off between lower inequality and higher growth (the so-called 'equity–efficiency' trade-off). Instead, it may be that government measures to make us more equal can also put us on a path of higher and more stable economic prosperity. I will return to this in Chapter 4, where I set out what we should do to reduce the high levels of inequality in the UK.

Claim: high levels of inequality reduce social mobility, and make it impossible to have equality of opportunity

It is an entirely natural reaction for parents to want to give their children the best start in life and to provide as many opportunities as possible for them to go on to live a happy, healthy and successful life. But it is not hard to realise that the ability of parents to provide these opportunities varies enormously between those with a lot of resources and those with a little. As a result, you will not be surprised to learn that children of affluent parents are more likely to do well at school than children from less well-off families. And this is one of the mechanisms that explains why inequalities can perpetuate: without the conscious intervention of governments – and I will argue in Chapter 4 that there is much that governments can do – inequalities in one generation lead to inequalities in the next.

Figure 2.2 illustrates this phenomenon, using data from Claire Crawford, Lindsey Macmillan and Anna Vignoles that tracks where children in England with different socio-economic backgrounds scored, on average, in standardised tests that children do throughout school (instead of the actual score, the figure shows the ranking, from 0 to 100, and so the average child would score 50, and the child with the highest score would get 100). Children from the least deprived fifth of families score, on average, considerably more in these tests (and in the compulsory exams sat at 16 or 18) than children from the most deprived fifth, and this gap grows as children age. There is some scope to debate the relative importance of nature and nurture, but there is simply no way that innate differences between children can explain all the variation seen here.

We do not yet have the complete explanation for what it is that more advantaged parents do to help their children thrive, but it will include things like spending more on their children's education or other activities, giving or lending their children money at key life stages, or using connections and contacts to help their children get ahead. Indeed, if you start to list all the things that can help children thrive at school and in life generally,

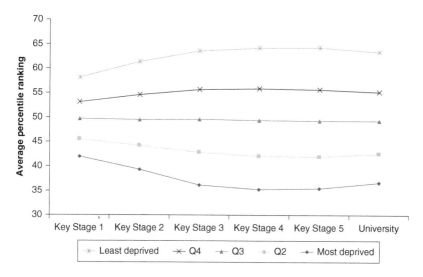

Figure 2.2   Average percentile rankings at each stage of English children's educational trajectory, by socio-economic status (measured in quintiles)

Source: Based on data underpinning Figure 1 in Crawford et al. (2017)

it is hard to think of any that are not easier to provide, in general, with a higher income.[40]

Having done well at school, children of affluent parents typically go on to get jobs that pay well. If family background played no role in determining how successful people grow up to be, then there would be little relation between my earnings and my parents' earnings, and we would say that such a society has a high degree of intergenerational social mobility. But if there is a close relationship between a child's earnings and their parents' earnings, then this shows that there is social *immobility*. We now have estimates of the relationship between children's earnings and their parents' earnings from many countries. What is particularly alarming is the fact that *how closely a child's earnings are related to their parents' earnings* seems to be (positively) related to *the level of inequality when the child was growing up*, as can be seen from the pattern shown in Figure 2.3: the countries that are more unequal are those with less social mobility.[41]

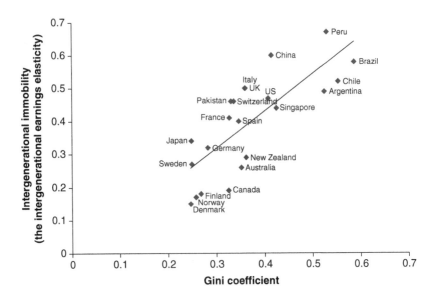

Figure 2.3 The 'Great Gatsby curve'

Source: Based on data underpinning Figure 2 of Corak (2013b)

This work reveals that it is not the United States that is the land of opportunity, where pluck, hard work and grit will give you your just rewards; quite the opposite – it's Sweden! (If you are born in the United States and hope to grow up to be healthy, wealthy and wise, then your best hope is to be born into a healthy, wealthy and wise family.) And cross-national research confirms the findings of studies from the United States or the UK: the relationship is due to the way that parents help their children gain educational qualifications, which then make it easier for children to grow up as high earners, and that parents are more likely to do this where inequality is high, because then there is more at stake.[42]

We also know that social mobility in the UK has declined as income inequality has risen. Figure 2.4 tracks children who were born in 1958 – and who grew up in the relatively equal 1960s and 1970s – and those born in 1970 – who left compulsory education as income inequality in

background

the UK was reaching its peak. The figure shows what fraction of children managed to reach different quintiles (fifths) of the income distribution, analysed separately according to what quintiles of the income distribution their parents were in. The conclusions are very clear at the top and bottom of the income distribution: children who grew up in high-income families are much more likely to be high income themselves as adults than other children, and children who grew up in low-income families are much more likely to be low income themselves as adults. The pattern is true for children born in 1958 and 1970, but it is stronger in 1970: your background has more influence where you end up for children born in 1970 than those born in 1958. Social mobility seems to be falling.

Economist Raj Chetty and colleagues have recently been using vast quantities of data on the earnings of adults and their parents in the United States, and find big falls over time in social mobility. They estimated that

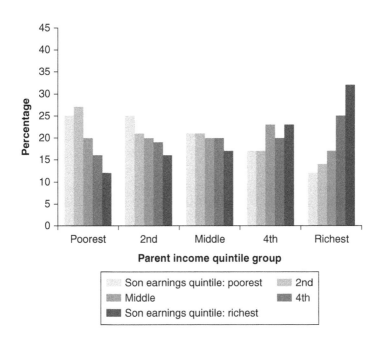

Figure 2.4a Intergenerational mobility in the 1958 birth cohort

33

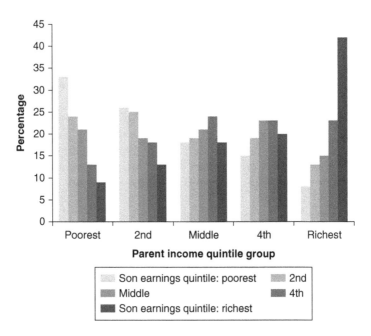

Figure 2.4b Intergenerational mobility in the 1970 birth cohort

Source: Based on data underpinning Figures 0.1 and 0.2 in Elliot Major and Machin (2018)

about 9 out of every 10 children born in the United States in the 1940s would grow up to earn more than their parents, but this is only true for about half of those born in the 1980s.[43] This is a measure of absolute social mobility, rather than relative social mobility. But Chetty and colleagues show that this big fall is not due to a fall in economic growth, but to the fact that more and more of the gains from growth are being captured by those at the top.

These links between inequality and social mobility are extremely important. We might be more tolerant of inequality if it was transient, or if every child in the next new generation had an equal chance at getting to the top. But they do not. Indeed, it seems that the more inequality there is in society, the more that our future life-chances are constrained by – or protected by – our family background, and that does not seem fair.

Claim: wealth inequalities are set to grow and produce a new super-wealthy inheritance class

In his ground-breaking book *Capital in the Twenty-First Century* (2014 for the English edition), economist Thomas Piketty presented data for many countries over decades and centuries to chart the way in which wealth inequalities perpetuate (he calls it 'capital', but by this he means financial wealth, i.e. money in bank accounts, stocks, shares in companies, pension funds and other financial instruments, and physical 'stuff', including housing). The book also contains an alarming prediction. Piketty argues that underlying economic forces mean that wealth will inevitably grow in importance in our economies and, if unchecked, some countries could end up resembling the situation at the beginning of the twentieth century – the so-called Gilded Age in the United States, or la Belle Epoque in Europe – where society is extremely divided and the very rich are dominated by those who live off their inherited wealth (UK readers might find it helpful to think of the first series of *Downton Abbey* on TV). Such a world, he says, would not be desirable. First, it affronts our sense of fairness if the easiest way to become rich is to be born to someone rich, rather than to study and work hard. Second, because the rich tend to have more of a voice in our political debates, policies and societal discourse, they will try to defend the interests of inherited wealth in ways that will be harmful to the rest of society.

This last point is echoed in arguments made by Joseph Stiglitz, who is very critical of the relationship between high levels of inequality and politics. His fundamental argument is that 'The economic elite have pushed for a [legal] framework that benefits them at the expense of the rest … [Our] inequality gets reflected in every important decision that we make as a nation [… and …] these decisions themselves help perpetuate and exacerbate this inequality.' His argument is about the United States, and reflects several things that are unique to, or particularly pronounced in, the United States, including the role of campaign finance ('[I]ncreasingly, and especially in the United States, it seems that the political system is more akin to "one dollar one vote" than to "one person one vote"'[44]), the very large number of corporate lobbyists, and the free flow of individuals from political posts to the corporate world and back again. It is not clear whether his argument applies with full force in other countries, but it highlights another way that inequality can perpetuate. If the very rich can obtain power – of any sort – or influence decisions through their wealth without enough checks and balances in the system, then they have the opportunity to influence society in ways that make it easier for them to accumulate more wealth, and harder for others to join them at the top.

r > g

Piketty's economic reasoning has been summarised by the expression $r > g$, where r is the return on capital and g is the growth rate of the economy. If the economy grows more slowly than the rate of return on capital, then more of our national income will go to people who own capital, rather than to those who earn an income by working. Because people who own capital tend to be well off, then they will save a lot of their income or be able to achieve high returns, and so they will accumulate more wealth, worsening inequality.

Piketty argues that $r > g$ is the usual historical state of affairs but that, crucially, there have been two long periods during the twentieth century when $r < g$. The first period spans the two world wars and the Great Depression in between. These events dramatically equalised the distribution of capital, either because capital was physically destroyed (definitely true in parts of continental Europe), or because its value was reduced by inflation or policy measures that governments implemented to pay off war debts. In effect, this period saw r, the rate of return on capital, fall to very low levels. The second period was from the Second World War to the 1970s, during which time many developed countries' economies grew very quickly, meaning that g was especially high, and the returns to capital were often taxed very heavily (including an infamous 98% tax rate on income from financial investments in the UK in the 1970s), such that an after-tax measure of r was especially low. During these times, then, the pressures towards ever-growing inequality were not apparent. But, since about the 1980s, Piketty argues, economic growth in the developed economies, g, has begun to slow, and taxes on capital, inheritances and the very rich have been cut, increasing a post-tax measure of r, and we have returned to the more normal situation where $r > g$ (see Figure 2.5).

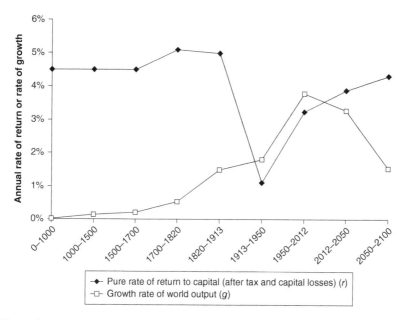

Figure 2.5   After-tax rate of return (*r*) and growth rate (*g*)

Source: Data underpinning Figure 10.10 in Piketty (2014), available from
http://piketty.pse.ens.fr/en/capital21c2

Piketty's book was a monumental undertaking. It contains the results of painstaking work using historical sources to estimate the amount of capital and inheritances, and wealth and income inequality, over decades or centuries. The book also contains some predictions that are not supported by existing theories, and puts forward ideas which go against established ideas in economics. It has therefore attracted a great deal of comment and criticism.[45]

Some have questioned whether *r* will continue indefinitely to be greater than *g*, given that most economic theories say that as the amount of wealth in the economy grows, the return to it (i.e. *r*) should fall.[46] Piketty does not think it will, based on his historical evidence that *r* has remained at 4–5% through most of post-medieval economic history, but he does not have an explanation for why this has happened. But others have argued that $r > g$ is irrelevant for explaining the growing importance of wealth and rising wealth inequalities: what matters is that the very wealthy save a lot and can get a higher return on their investments than the less wealthy.[47]

Piketty's story about how the very rich ensure that their successors also grow up to be rich relies heavily on inheritances of wealth coming to dominate the top of the wealth and income distribution. As I will show in Chapter 3, most of the income of those with the highest incomes comes from the labour market, not from unearned income derived from wealth, although difficulties in measuring incomes at the very top means this is an area of active debate.[48] And two omissions from Piketty's book are that it has little to say about why income from employment is so unequally distributed (other than some idea about the very top earners, which I discuss in Chapter 3), and it says little about all the things that parents do other than bequeath or transfer wealth to help their children thrive, as I discussed earlier in this chapter.[49]

But the key facts presented by Piketty are not in dispute: income inequality is on the rise in most developed countries, especially among the very rich. Wealth is growing in importance in many developed economies, and this is putting pressure on inequality, because wealth is more unequally distributed than income. At the very least, Piketty's predictions should be taken as a warning about one possible state of the future world. Wealth and income used to be more unequally distributed, and there are reasons to think that, after a long period in which economics and governments reduced the importance of wealth, we are now in a less benign economic environment.

Conclusion

This chapter has taken a tour through the new arguments that high levels of inequality are damaging our society and economy. There is evidence – not yet conclusive – that inequalities are actively harmful to society and that, left to their own devices, inequalities perpetuate through a whole series of economic, political and social processes, including so-called 'opportunity hoarding' by affluent parents seeking the best for their children. And doubts are emerging that government measures to reduce inequality end up slowing down economic growth: indeed, inequality itself may be a brake on growth. These questions are not yet settled, but there could be more reasons than just envy to wish that resources were shared out a little more equally. With this in mind, the next chapter sets out what we know about economic inequalities in the UK.

what do we know about inequality?

In the Introduction – see especially Figure 1.6 – I gave an overview of economic inequality in the UK over the last few decades. In this chapter, I will explore these trends in detail. I will explain why income inequality rose so much through the 1980s, why it hardly changed at all in the 1990s and 2000s, and what is behind the unusual path that inequality has taken since 2008. The most important sources of income for households are earnings from employment, so I will look in some detail at what has happened to inequality in wages and earnings, and how changing working patterns have affected income inequality. I will also show what impact changes to personal taxes and social security benefits have had on income inequality. With new analysis of administrative data on tax returns, I will zoom in to see what we know about the very rich in the UK. I will show that the data that underpins the most common estimates of income inequality misses out on some of the highest incomes in the UK, and that, although the very rich in the UK did get hit by the financial crisis, they have now recovered so that the fraction of national income going to the richest 0.01% (about 5,300 adults) has almost regained its historical high point. The chapter ends by looking at inequality in household wealth, and assessing Thomas Piketty's prediction that growing wealth inequalities and inheritances are set to return the UK to levels of inequality last seen at the start of the twentieth century.

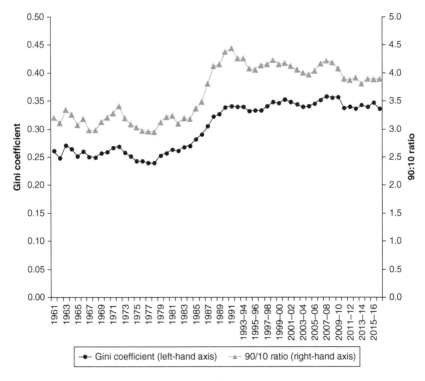

Figure 3.1 Income inequality in the UK, 1961 to present

Source: www.ifs.org.uk/uploads/publications/bns/bn19_figs.xlsx

Income inequality

Figure 3.1 shows the Gini coefficient and the 90:10 ratio for household income in Great Britain since 1961, with the Gini coefficient measured on the left-hand axis and the 90:10 on the right (go back to the Introduction if you want reminding what the Gini coefficient and the 90:10 ratio are). The figure begins in 1961, as that is the earliest date for which there is consistent data on household disposable income, although alternative estimates with other concepts of income suggest that income inequality now is higher than it has been since at least 1937.[50] Estimates of income inequality in 2017–18 were released as this book was being finalised, and are not shown here, but are no different from those in 2016–17.[51]

Over this period, the Gini coefficient tells a story in three acts. The first act, from 1961 to the early 1980s, was the UK's low-inequality period, with the Gini coefficient wobbling about 0.25. In act 2, from the late 1970s to 1990, inequality rose by about 10 percentage points. Act 3, which began in 1990, is the high-inequality period, with the Gini coefficient wobbling around 0.35. (You should not make too much of the 'wobbles' in the series. We do not know the income of every household in the UK, so the best we can do is *estimate* the amount of inequality. This means that we cannot be sure whether small wobbles in the level, like we have seen since 1990, capture true changes, or just reflect that the estimates are more accurate in some years than others.) I showed in the Introduction – see Figure 1.7 – that the UK has the second highest level of inequality among the G7 countries with the seven largest economies behind the United States, and has the second highest across all European countries.

From 1961 to the early 1990s, the 90:10 measure told a similar story to the Gini: unchanging inequality until the early 1980s and then a rapid rise. But having peaked in the early 1990s, the 90:10 measure has been declining slowly since. This is a helpful reminder that there is no single, perfect measure of inequality, and that sometimes we can come to different conclusions using inequality measures that put weight on different parts of the income distribution. The two measures together show that we have become more equal since 1990 across most of the income distribution, but not at the extremes.

Why has income inequality in the UK changed over time?

The level of income inequality that the UK had in the mid-1970s would put it among the most equal countries in the world nowadays. So how did income inequality go up by so much in the 1980s? And why did it stop rising in the early 1990s?

To help with this, Figure 3.2 shows the pattern of income growth across the income distribution in five periods: 1977 to 1990; 1990 to 1997; 2000 to 2007; 2007 to 2011; 2011 to 2016. The underpinning data does not track the same individuals over time; instead, to draw the line for (say) the 1977 to 1990 period, I compared each centile of the income distribution in 1977 with the same centile in 1990, and calculated the average annual real-terms growth rate. If a line is sloping upwards as we move from left to right on the chart, then it means that higher incomes were growing faster than were lower incomes, and this would push inequality up; if a line is sloping downwards as we move from left to right, then it means that lower incomes were catching up with those on higher incomes, and this would push inequality down.

I will first give an overview of the changes over these periods. I will then look in some detail at how and why the distribution of earnings has changed, and how this has affected income inequality, and then at the impact on inequality of changes to the tax system and to social security benefits.

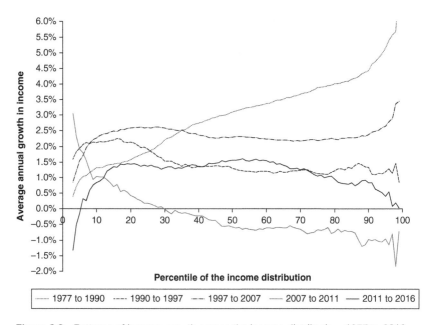

Figure 3.2 Patterns of income growth across the income distribution, 1977 to 2016

Source: Based on data provided by the Institute for Fiscal Studies. See also Figure 3.10 in Cribb et al. (2018)

Why did inequality rise so much during the 1980s?

Income inequality rose in many other developed economies in the 1980s and 1990s, but the 10 percentage point rise in the Gini coefficient in the UK in the 1980s is one of the largest and fastest rises on record. In Figure 3.2, the line for 1977 to 1990 slopes unambiguously upwards; in other words, whichever part of the income distribution we look at, incomes were growing faster for the rich than for the poor.

The huge rise in income inequality was due to a combination of techno-logical changes, global economic circumstances and policy choices made by UK governments that all affected the sort of jobs being done and how well they were paid.[52] As a result, well-paid people saw large pay rises, and lower-paid people saw smaller rises (I will explore this in detail in the next section). At the same time, the tax system did less to slow this down – the top rate of income tax was cut from 73% to 40% – and the social security system left those out of work further behind, mainly because benefits were increased in line with growth in prices, rather than growth in earnings. Other changes in the 1980s were that income from self-employment and income from investments both grew in importance, became more unequally distrib-uted, and tended to be received by those who already had high incomes. Income from pensions also grew in importance – as more and more people retired with some form of private pension – but income from pen-sions became more equally distributed.[53]

Why did inequality stop rising in 1990?

Figure 3.1 showed that the Gini coefficient has hardly changed since 1990, but the patterns of income growth in Figure 3.2 tell us that this (relatively) unchanging Gini happened not because the income distribu-tion stayed the same shape (which would correspond to a line that was close to horizontal in Figure 3.2). Instead, changes in different parts of the income distribution pushed inequality in different directions, with an overall effect that was close to zero. For example, between 1990 and 1997, Figure 3.2 shows that incomes became more equal between (roughly) the 10th and 80th centile (which would reduce inequality), but that the bottom 10% fell behind the second decile group (which would push inequality up). Similarly, between 1997 and 2007, incomes became more equal between (roughly) the 25th and 75th centiles, but inequalities grew below the 25th centile and above the 75th centile, with particularly strong income growth at the 98th and 99th centiles.

Research suggests that the same forces pushing inequality up in the 1980s – changes to work patterns and rising earnings inequality – would have continued to push income inequality up during the 1990s and 2000s, albeit at a slower rate.[54] The reason that income inequality has not risen since 1991 is because other factors have been pushing it down. Income from financial investments (which is very unequally distributed) became slightly less important, and income from private pensions became more widespread. Steady economic growth meant unemployment fell from its high point in the mid-1980s, and social and policy changes meant single parents were more likely to be in paid work than they were in 1990. Meanwhile, governments through the 1990s and 2000s increased social security benefits for people aged 60 or over and families with young children. All together, this meant that groups which historically have had low incomes were able to catch up with the rest of society. On the other hand, there was rapid income growth in incomes at the top of the top decile group during the 2000s.

What did the financial crisis, Great Recession and a near-decade of austerity do?

The path of income inequality since the financial crisis of 2008 has been unusual.[55] Inequality tends to rise when the economy is growing, because people who are in paid work see incomes rise and so pull ahead of those who do not work or who are retired. When the economy does poorly, this process reverses and inequality tends to fall. This is exactly what happened in the immediate aftermath of the financial crisis in 2008: some people lost their jobs, and they tended to come from previously middle- to high-income families, which reduced inequality. Meanwhile, those receiving state benefits saw their incomes rise, as part of a Labour government policy to pump-prime the economy and protect the poorest: this reduced inequality even more (Figure 3.2 shows that the strongest income growth between 2007 and 2011 was found among those with the lowest incomes).

But inequality since 2011 has not taken the path we would expect to see during an economic recovery. This reflects that both the recovery and government policy decisions since 2011 have been far from usual. In this recovery, average earnings have grown very slowly – adjusting for inflation, average earnings were no higher in December 2018 than they were at their pre-downturn peak[56] – and this has meant that the well-paid have not accelerated away. Furthermore, wages among low earners have grown by more than the average (thanks to increases in the minimum wage), the fraction of people in paid work has continued to rise, and low-waged workers have tended to work longer hours: all these have acted to reduce inequality, as those towards the bottom of the income distribution have been catching up with the rest. But the return to a growing economy in 2011 did not mean an end to government austerity, and more years of cuts to the generosity of social security benefits and tax credits have lowered incomes for those households towards the bottom, thus pushing inequality up. The combined effect is that the middle of the income distribution has pulled away from the bottom since 2011 – due to higher employment and benefit cuts – and the middle has been catching up with those towards the top – because of the weak growth in earnings. Unusually, then, headline measures of inequality have hardly changed since 2011, and they remain lower than they were before the financial crisis hit in 2008.

A focus on the labour market

Figure 3.3 shows how inequality in hourly wage rates, weekly earnings and annual earnings in the UK have changed since 1975.[57] For all three measures, inequality began to grow in 1975. Inequality in hourly wages peaked in the early 2000s, and inequality in weekly or annual earnings seems to have peaked at the start of the current decade.

Some of the rise in hourly wage inequality from the late 1970s is attributed to factors specific to the UK. The economic policy of Conservative governments in the 1980s was all about 'supply-side' reforms, including removing business regulations, particularly in the financial sector, and privatising state-run businesses. This increased freedom to operate, and power to the private sector is thought to have acted as a spur to high levels of pay for the well off.[58] Meanwhile, policy was also changed to weaken the powers of trade unions, which traditionally had worked to keep earnings up for their members; at its peak in 1980, just over half of workers were in a trade union, and it is now

Figure 3.3 Earnings inequality in the UK, 1975 to 2017–18

Source: Based on data provided by the Resolution Foundation. See also Box 2 of D'Arcy (2018)

just under a quarter.[59] But many other countries also saw earnings grow more unequal at this time, and the culprits are thought to be a combination of skill-biased technological change and globalisation. Why did these make us more unequal?

The idea behind 'skill-biased technical change' is that technological developments since the 1970s – broadly speaking, the revolution in information and communications technology (ICT), caused by falls in the cost of computer processing power – mean that less skilled workers have become less valuable (because what they are doing can be automated or replaced) but more skilled workers have become more valuable (because new technology allows them to achieve more). For example, a large supermarket chain with self-scan checkouts has less need for cashiers, but more need for data scientists (who can turn the data being captured into profit-winning sales strategies or logistics solutions). Self-driving trucks will mean less demand for hauliers, but more for software engineers. It is not inevitable that technological progress always works to the disadvantage of the low skilled (the plough, for example, was a fantastic innovation for an unskilled agricultural labourer), but this is the form that the ICT revolution is taking.[60]

'Globalisation' refers to a whole host of factors affecting international trade and corporate practices, including the revolution in manufacturing industry and export activity in China and elsewhere; the fact that, globally, trade barriers are falling; and the fact that financial capital, firms and the very rich have all become internationally mobile. Increased global trade is good for us, on balance, as consumers (although one could write another book analysing that claim), but, combined with the ease in which companies can offshore their services or use factories from all over the world, it can threaten us as workers. As it happens, globalisation has tended to exacerbate the impacts of skill-biased technological change: the two working together means that some workers are a lot less valuable in the UK, because what they do can be automated, or replaced with computer processing, or outsourced to a country where it can be done cheaper, or just not needed because firms have gone bust in the face of cheaper competition from overseas. At the same time, there has been an increase in poorly paid jobs in areas that are less vulnerable to technological change (because the tasks undertaken are hard to automate), or subject to fewer pressures from globalisation (because the workers are producing a service which cannot be done by workers overseas, such as retail, carework, security services); this trend is known as 'polarisation'.

The combination of all these factors led to inequality in hourly wages growing more or less continuously through the 1980s and through the 1990s (albeit more slowly). Since the start of the 2000s, wages in the top half of the distribution have continued to grow more unequal, but wages at the bottom have broadly kept pace with the rest. The most important factor explaining this has been the UK's National Minimum Wage, introduced in 1999; this shows that policy can make a real difference, and I will return to this in the next chapter.

How the labour market affects income inequality depends not just on inequality in hourly wages, but also on who in the household is working and how many hours a week they work. In general, weekly earnings have been changing in a way that means that top earners have continued to pull away from the middle, but the bottom of the distribution of weekly earnings has caught up with the middle. And looking at the sort of people who are changing their work patterns reveals that these changes in labour market behaviour have increased inequalities in household income (especially so when also considering earnings from self-employment). This is because lower-paid men now work less than they used to and lower-paid women now work more than they used to, on average, and the sort of women who are now working more tend to live in households where someone else works.[61]

The role of changes to the tax system and social security benefits

Given the unprecedentedly large rise in income inequality during the 1980s, Tom Clark and Andrew Leicester were interested in discovering how much was due to changes to the tax and benefit system.[62] Slightly frustratingly, the answer turns out to depend on what you mean by 'a change' (or rather, what would count as 'no change' to taxes and benefits). If you think that increasing tax allowances and social security benefits each year in line with price inflation should count as 'no change', then changes to taxes through the 1980s and 1990s made us less equal, but changes to social security benefits made us more equal, with the combined impact on the Gini being approximately nothing (they estimate that reforms introduced by the Conservative governments of 1979 to 1997 would have increased the Gini by 1.1 percentage points, compared with the alternative of increasing tax allowances and benefits in line with prices).

But that might not be the best way to think about 'no change to the tax and benefit system'. Earnings usually grow faster than prices (except since 2008!), so if tax allowances are increased each year only in line with inflation, then more people will be paying tax on more of their earnings each year (this is known as 'fiscal drag'). If the value of benefits only rises each year in line with prices, then people who depend on income from state benefits will find themselves falling further behind those who are in work. In the long run, if governments increased tax allowances and cash benefits only in line with inflation, then we would have ever-rising inequality and ever-growing tax revenues. That is an odd notion of 'no change'.

A different way to think about a world in which there are 'no changes' to the tax and benefit system is one where tax allowances rise each year in line with growth in average earnings – which should prevent the fiscal drag I mentioned above – and where cash benefits did likewise – which should stop those on state benefits from falling behind. If this is our concept of 'nothing changing', then the research finds that changes to taxes and benefits from 1979 to 1997 *increased* the Gini coefficient by about 5 percentage points, or about half the rise seen over this period. This way of thinking about policy changes would lead us to conclude that taxes in the UK were cut for the better off throughout the 1980s and social security benefits were made gradually less generous. The result was the really large rise in inequality in a very short space of time. However, when the same exercise is done for the 1997–2010 Labour governments, it is clear that tax and benefit reforms acted to reduce inequality.

The record of the 2010–15 Coalition government is a little harder to characterise. Changes to taxes and social security benefits increased inequality in the bottom 80% (most people lost money through these reforms, because this was a period of austerity, but the poorest lost a greater fraction of their income), but they reduced inequality at the top because of a few measures (such as lowering the point where people start to pay the 40% income tax rate, and cuts to tax relief on pension saving) that targeted the richest decile group.[63] At the time of writing, tax and benefit changes announced by the two Conservative governments since 2015 have continued in the same vein.[64]

What do we know about those with the highest incomes?

All the statistics so far in this chapter are based on government-run surveys of thousands of households. This sort of data does not give accurate information on the circumstances of the very rich (see online **mikebrewereconomics.com/WDWK** for more on this), so researchers have recently started to use data from tax authorities instead.[65] The great thing about tax data is that we can focus in on the very richest people, and we do not have to worry about small sample sizes. The biggest drawback is that we need to believe that what those with very high incomes report to the tax authorities is the truth. Also, this data cannot be used to measure *total disposable income in a household* in the way we can with the survey data that underpins Figure 3.1, so the facts I report below all refer to individual-level taxable income, before deducting tax, and facts about the 'top 1%' refer to the richest 1% of all adults in the UK.[66]

How high are top incomes?

Table 3.1 reports new estimates of the scale of riches among the very rich from 2015–16 (the latest year available at the time of writing; this data is never up to date).[67] In 2015–16, anyone with an individual before-tax income of more than £42,200 was in the top 10% of adults (or the richest 5,360,000). To be in the top 1% (the richest 536,000), you would have needed three times as much, or at least £121,000 a year. [68] To be in the top 10% of the top 1% – and now we are down to the richest 53,600 adults – you would have needed an income above £513,000, or another four times higher. And the richest 10% of that group (i.e. the top 0.01%, or about the richest 5,360 people) all had incomes above £2,220,000. As Thomas Piketty said: '[t]he upper decile [group] is truly a world into

Table 3.1   Top incomes in the UK, 2015–16

To be in the top...	...you need to have an income of at least...	...and the average income in this group is...	Reminder: how many adults are in this group?
10%	£42,200	£87,800	5,360,000
10% but not the top 1%	£42,200	£61,700	4,820,000
1%	£121,000	£318,000	536,000
1% but not the top 0.1%	£121,000	£207,000	482,000
0.1%	£513,000	£1,320,000	53,600
0.1% but not the top 0.01%	£513,000	£892,000	48,200
0.01%	£2,220,000	£5,160,000	5,360

Source: Author's calculations based on Survey of Personal Incomes data. See Brewer and Sámano-Robles (2019)

itself. It includes some people whose income is just two or three times greater than the mean and others whose resources are ten or twenty times greater, if not more'[69].

Figure 3.4 shows what fraction of top incomes are from earned income (as opposed to income from financial investments) and how this has changed over time. The vast majority of income in the top 10%, and even in the top 1%, is from earned income: only within the top 0.1% (the richest 53,600 adults) does income from financial assets come to more than a fifth of total income.[70]

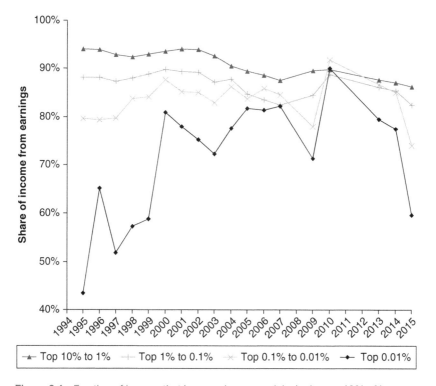

Figure 3.4 Fraction of income that is earned among adults in the top 10% of incomes in the UK

Source: Author's calculations based on Survey of Personal Incomes data. See Brewer and Sámano-Robles (2019)

What has happened to top income shares?

Figure 3.5 shows estimates of top income shares based on this tax data. The share of pre-tax income that goes to the richest 1% of adults was at its lowest level in 1978, at slightly under 6%. Like the Gini coefficient, this measure of inequality rose through the 1980s. Unlike the Gini coefficient, it continued to rise through the 1990s and the 2000s: in fact, the share of income going to the top 1% grew by more between 1990 and 2009 than it did in the 1980s. The share of income going to the top 0.1% went up by a half between 1996 and 2009, to reach 6.5%, or 65 times more than if we shared all income equally. In 2015, the richest 0.01% of adults had just over 2.4% of income, or 241 times as much as they would have if all income was shared equally. Top income shares have risen so much that,

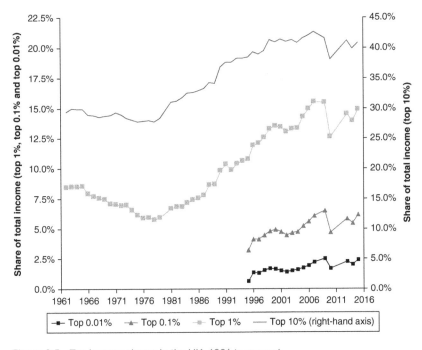

Figure 3.5 Top income shares in the UK, 1961 to present

Source: Before 1995: https://wid.world; after 1995: author's calculations based on Survey of Personal Incomes (see Brewer and Sámano-Robles, 2019) and data from wid.world

in 2009 (the least equal year on record, according to this data), the richest 0.1% had a larger share of national income than did the richest 1% in 1979 (the most equal year). Likewise, the top 1% in 2009 had more than did the top 10% in 1979.

Top income shares fell back considerably in 2009, after the financial crisis, partly because (as I will show) so many of the very rich work in the financial sector or receive income from financial investments, but also because of changes to the top rate of income tax in April 2010 and April 2013. The estimates since 2010 are missing for a couple of years, but we can now see a clear upward trend: by 2015–16, the share of income going to the top 0.1% was the second highest it had ever been, and the share of the top 1% was the fourth highest ever. And these top income shares are very high: among other rich economies in 2014, the fraction of income going to the top 1% in the UK was the second highest among developed countries, after the United States, which really leads the way here, with the richest 1% having a staggering 20% of all pre-tax income.[71]

As measures of inequality, these top income shares are telling a different story from the Gini coefficient and the 90:10 (both shown in Figure 3.1), which have hardly changed since the early 1990s and are lower now than immediately before the financial crisis. Careful forensic work by Stephen Jenkins and others has shown that the survey data that underpins Figure 3.1 underestimates the incomes of the very rich (and therefore underestimates inequality), even after a correction has been made that tries to solve the problem.[72] In particular, there is a sharp rise in top incomes between 2004 and 2007 that is missed entirely by the data underpinning the conventional estimates of the Gini, as shown in Figure 3.1. This is worrying. It suggests that the main source of data on income inequality in the UK is giving us inaccurate information on the changing circumstances of the very rich (and I will return to this in Chapter 4). It looks like we should modify the story about the recent trends in income inequality in the UK to one which recognises that, while gaps across most of the distribution are getting no worse, the very rich are continuing to pull slowly, inexorably, away.

Who are the 1% (and the 0.1%, and the 0.01%)?

Figures 3.6, 3.7 and 3.8 present new analysis showing the typical age of people in the richest 10%, where they live, and in what industries they work.[73]

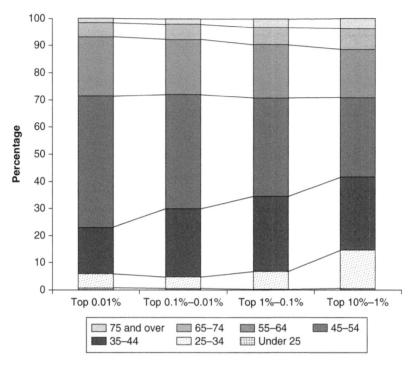

Figure 3.6 Age of the top 10 percent, 2013–16

Sources: Author's calculations based on Survey of Personal Incomes data. See Brewer and Sámano-Robles (2019)

The very rich are very likely to be between the ages of 45 and 65. About 1 in 6 of the richest 10% (5,360,000 adults) are under 35, but this is the case for only 1 in 20 of the richest 0.1% (the richest 53,600); incidentally those who are young and very rich are more likely than older, rich people to be working in arts, entertainment and recreation (which includes professional sportspeople) or to have no earned income. 28% of the richest 10% of adults are women, but only 19% of the richest 1% (536,000 adults) and 9% of the richest 0.01% (5,360 adults). Of the richest 0.1%, less than a quarter live outside London, south-east England and the east of England; over half of the richest 0.01% live in London.

Some jobs are common among what I will unscientifically call the 'comfortably well off' (those in the top 10% but not in the top 1%), but are unlikely to be found among those with higher incomes: these include education (which includes university professors) and those in manufacturing, who are in the top 10% but unlikely to be in the top 1%, and healthcare professionals, who are in the top 1%, but very unlikely to be in the top 0.1%. Other than those working in the arts, entertainment or in professional sports, who are over-represented in the richest 0.01%, the two industries which become more common as we focus on those with higher incomes are finance, insurance and real estate; and those providing professional, scientific and technical services (a category that includes lawyers and architects). Over half of

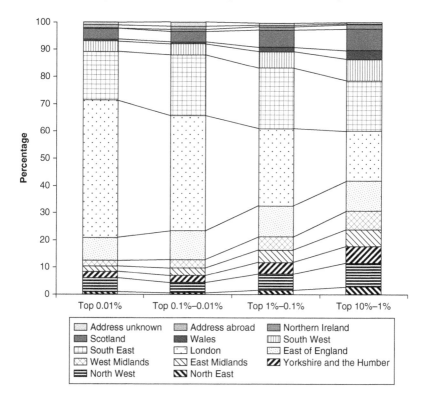

Figure 3.7   Region of residence of the top 10 percent, 2013–16

Sources: Author's calculations based on Survey of Personal Incomes data. See Brewer and Sámano-Robles (2019)

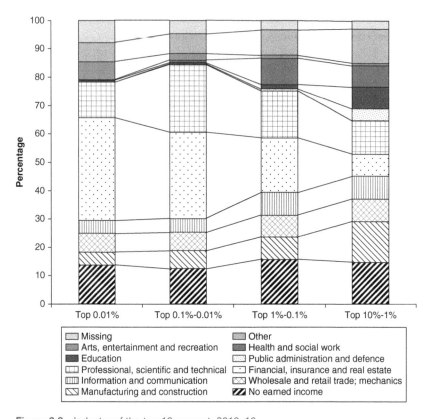

Figure 3.8 Industry of the top 10 percent, 2013–16

Sources: Author's calculations based on Survey of Personal Incomes data. See Brewer and Sámano-Robles (2019)

the top 0.1% work in these areas; other research has shown that 60% of the growth in top incomes between 1998 and 2007 went to people working in 'financial intermediation'.[74]

Why have top earnings been racing away?

Skill-biased technological change and globalisation, which are the main causes of the growing inequality in hourly wages through the 1980s and

1990s, do not explain why remuneration at the very top has been growing much faster than for the rest of us, nor why it has grown so much
faster in some countries than others. But there are other theories. What
is key to most is that the 'market' for managers and top executives (and
that is increasingly who are the top earners) does not work like the stylised textbook market that economics students learn about. In such a
world, there would be lots of firms and lots of top executives, and Adam
Smith's 'invisible hand' would guide the market to a situation where
executives were paid what they were worth (where 'what they are worth'
reflected how much they contributed to a firm's profits; this is sometimes
known as 'marginal productivity theory'). Firms that offered executives
less than this would find that staff leave to go work elsewhere, and firms
that offered executives too much would find themselves swamped with
applicants, or have angry shareholders demanding to know where the
profits have gone.

But this is not what is happening. The core of the problem is that
it is impossible for firms to judge the worth of a senior manager or
executive before he is hired (I showed earlier that it is usually a 'he'),
and not much easier to do so afterwards. This means there is a large
gap between the minimum pay that an executive would accept and the
maximum that the company would be prepared to hand over, so there
is scope for bargaining to take place.[75] As it is time consuming and
expensive to hire senior people, and there can be a lot at stake (the fortunes of the whole company, in the case of the CEO or UK equivalent),
this tends to give the bargaining power to the managers and executives, rather than to the firms.

People have pointed to additional failings. As Piketty says: 'in
practice, the invisible hand does not exist … and the market is always
embodied in specific institutions such as corporate hierarchies and
compensation committees'. As Piketty suggests, the pay of senior managers and executives is usually set by compensation or remuneration
committees who are asked to make an assessment of what should be
paid given the 'market rate'. But there is no such thing as the 'market rate': there is just a small number of individual agreements, mostly
made on the basis of advice of other remuneration committees, who
themselves have been looking at the mythical 'market rate', and so on,
and so on, in an ever-lasting recursive spiral. (This is not helped by the
fact that many members of remuneration committees are former senior

executives, leading to 'a cartel of high-level managers who give each other excessively high incomes'.)[76] It gets worse if no firm wants to be seen to be paying below the market rate, or no executive wants to admit to being below average performance: if all firms and managers want to be in the top half of the pay distribution, then that ever-lasting recursive spiral will start spiralling upwards. A final problem is that when remuneration committees set pay deals, they are not spending their own money but that of the company, and this is ultimately owned by the shareholders, who find it hard to have any influence on these decisions. The UK does have a requirement that shareholders approve a company's remuneration policy, but these policies cover only the formal company directors, who are only a handful of employees in each firm.

If these theories are true, then, at best, some at the top are being paid considerably more than what they are worth to the firm; at worst, as Piketty alleges, 'top managers have the power by and large to set their own remuneration'. In Chapter 2, I discussed Stiglitz's arguments that pay at the top is racing away not because top managers are helping their employers become more profitable or efficient, but because they are negotiating themselves a larger portion of their employer's profits, or making personal gains at someone else's expense. Furthermore, Stiglitz argues that low tax rates at the top actively encourage this sort of behaviour, by making it more rewarding than it would be in a world with high income tax rates to go to the effort to extract more pay from the company.

There are counter-arguments, and some argue that very high levels of pay are the result of well-functioning markets.[77] One idea is that the 'economics of superstars' now applies to senior executives and top managers. Newer theories explore the idea that the larger the firm, the more scope there is for a good CEO to make a difference (or to flip this round: the larger the firms, the more they will be prepared to pay to reduce the risk that a bad CEO bankrupts the firm).[78] Some argue that, in technology companies, some of the super-high salaries reflect the difficulty that firms have in capturing all of the innovative ideas made by their employees.[79] But even if the very high levels of compensation are the outcomes of fair markets (as economists understand them), this still does not mean that these negotiations are producing the best outcomes for *society*, for the reasons I outlined in Chapter 2.

So do employers pay their top managers and CEOs too much? Or do they get back what they pay for? Well, research continues, but it is even harder for researchers to work out whether any one top manager or executive is good for a company, or for our economy, than it is for their employer. We do know that there is a very strong (negative) link between the top rate of income tax and what share of a country's pre-tax income goes to the very rich: cuts to top rates of income tax tend to go alongside increases in the share of a country's pre-tax income that goes to the very rich. Of course, if top rates of income tax were cut, then the very rich would certainly end up receiving a greater share of *post-tax* income than before. But what we actually see is that, when top tax rates fall, the *pre-tax* pay packets of the very rich go up: they get paid more, and they pay less tax. It could be argued that this is entirely in line with standard textbook economics: by reducing top tax rates – as the UK and the United States did in the 1980s – the very rich get to keep more of what they earn, and so (one might argue) they have a larger incentive to work hard and innovate. This may be true, but it is also very hard to find any sort of link between the top rate of tax and a country's economic performance.[80] In other words, cutting top rates of tax does not seem to make the pie any bigger, but instead intensifies the activities of the very rich to obtain themselves a larger share of the same-size pie at the expense of everyone else, fully in line with Stiglitz's ideas. I will return to this in Chapter 4.

How has wealth inequality in the UK changed over time?

It is harder to get accurate data on the distribution of wealth than it is for income. The most comprehensive data for the UK comes from the Wealth and Assets Survey run by the Office for National Statistics (the ONS).[81] This shows huge inequalities in wealth holdings: in 2014–16, the 10th centile of the household wealth distribution was £13,600, the median household had £259,400, and the 90th centile was £1,210,000, giving a 90:10 ratio of 89. And this gives rise to some eye-watering wealth shares, as can be read off from Figure 3.9, which shows the Lorenz curve for income and for wealth (read the Introduction if you would like a reminder of what is a Lorenz curve). The ONS estimates that the wealthiest 10% of households own 44% of the total wealth in the UK. This is twice as much as the next wealthiest 2,600,000 households, and more wealth than the least wealthy 80% of households (all 20.7 million of them) put together. The Gini coefficient for UK household wealth in 2014–16 was 0.62, and average (mean) wealth was £493,000, so if a succession of pairs of UK households compared wealth levels, then the difference on average would be over £611,000.

Figure 3.10 shows the ways in which UK households in different parts of the wealth distribution hold their wealth. Of the £12,730,000,000,000 (that is just under £13 trillion) of household wealth in the UK (measured

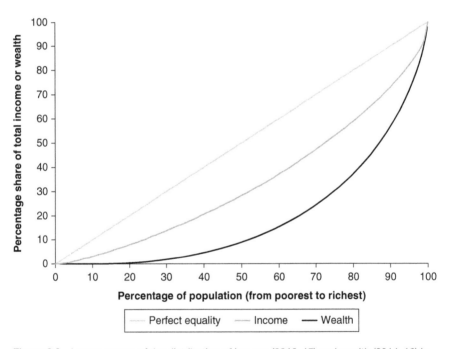

Figure 3.9 Lorenz curves of the distribution of income (2016–17) and wealth (2014–16) in the UK

Sources: Income: Based on data provided by the Institute for Fiscal Studies, derived from the 'Households Below Average Income' data-set. Wealth: Based on Table 2.7 of ONS (2018a)

in 2014–16), 42% was private pension wealth, 35% was property, 13% money financial assets and 10% was physical assets (which includes a household's possessions, the most important of which for many will be vehicles and jewellery).[82] Of these, physical wealth is the most equally distributed, and financial wealth is the most unequally distributed. For the wealthiest 30% of households, private pensions are the largest single source of wealth; for households in the middle of the wealth distribution, property wealth is the most important source; and for households towards the bottom, physical wealth is the most

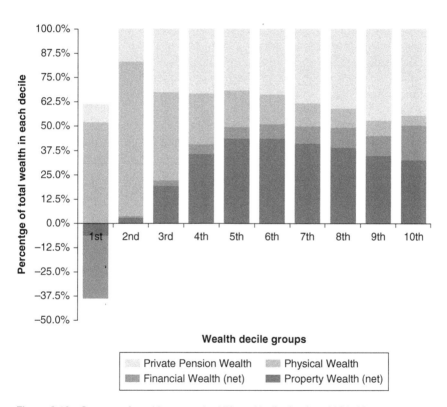

Figure 3.10 Sources of wealth across the UK wealth distribution, 2014–16

Source: Based on Table 2.3 of ONS (2018a)

important (but what you cannot tell from Figure 3.11 is that the wealthier you are, the more of each sort of wealth you are likely to have). There is a clichéd image of a capital-rich, income-poor individual eking out an existence on a meagre income in a house worth millions. Such people may exist, but the overwhelming tendency is for those with high wealth also to have high levels of income (and vice versa). Among the 10% (2,545,000) of households with the lowest income, the median level of wealth is £31,900, a lower figure than in every other income decile group; among the 10% of households with the highest income, the median level of wealth is just over £1 million.

Looking internationally, the OECD thinks that the UK is about mid-table across rich economies for levels of wealth inequality.[83] If anything, given how unequally distributed incomes are in the UK, it is a little surprising that the Gini for wealth is not even higher. Among those for which we have reliable data, the most unequal country is, once more, the United States, where the wealthiest 10% have almost 80% of all wealth.

There are, however, good reasons to think that the Wealth and Assets Survey (WAS) underestimates inequality in household wealth because the underlying sample does not accurately capture the wealth of very wealthy people (for similar reasons to why the data on household incomes used for the series in Figure 3.1 misses out on the income of the very rich).[84] This becomes clear when looking at estimates of how wealth inequality has changed over time. Figure 3.11 shows several estimates of top wealth shares, based on a variety of data sources.

Piketty estimated that wealth inequality in the UK reached its peak in the early twentieth century, when the wealthiest 10% of households owned over 90% of all wealth (and the wealthiest 1% owned over two-thirds). He estimates that wealth inequality then fell, bottoming out between about 1970 and 1990, since when wealth has become steadily, if slowly, more unequally distributed. Piketty's estimates have been challenged: we can see that his estimates for top wealth shares in recent years are far higher than those from the WAS, the source of the data underpinning Figures 3.9 and 3.10 and the facts presented earlier in this section, but they are also higher than those of other researchers. Piketty thinks that data on wealth that comes from administrative information on estates (the amount of wealth bequeathed when people die) is a more

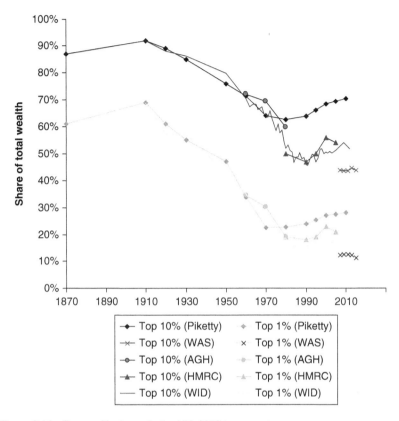

Figure 3.11 Top wealth shares in the UK, 1870 to present

Sources: Piketty: Figure 10.3 in Piketty (2014); WAS: Table 2.7 of ONS (2018a); AGH and HMRC: Figure 2.5 in Hills et al. (2013); WID: downloaded from wid.world. Some data points have been interpolated

reliable guide to the true distribution of wealth than the WAS. On the other hand, various adjustments needs to be made to this estates data (to reflect that the amount of wealth one has affects how likely one is to die, and that people usually make efforts to avoid inheritance tax, and so on), and differences in those adjustments seem to be the reason why Piketty's estimates are higher than those made by others. But all the series seem to agree that inequality in wealth stopped falling in the 1970s, and is probably higher now than 40 years ago.[85]

But whatever the actual level of wealth inequality, what is undisputed is that the total amount of wealth held by UK households has been rising. Using data from a source that underestimates household wealth, John Hills and colleagues find that, between 1995 and 2005, the amount of household wealth at the median rose from £37,000 to £100,000, and the amount at the 90th centile rose from £190,000 to £390,000 (all in 2005 prices). The amount of wealth held by the 50th centile did grow at a faster rate than the 90th centile (and this data does suggest that top wealth shares fell over this period), but the gap between households at the 50th and the 90th centile of the distribution rose from £153,000 to £290,000. That does not feel like a more equal distribution.

One response to this is to monitor directly *absolute* inequalities in wealth – like that £290,000 difference between the 50th and the 90th centile.[86] I prefer, though, the approach suggested by John Hills and colleagues, which is to relate differences in wealth to typical levels of earnings. For example, if person A has £1,000,000 of wealth and person B has £10,000 and an income of £25,000, then person B would have to save their entire income for just under 40 years to amass as much wealth as person A (ignoring interest rates, inflation, etc.). If person A's wealth goes up by £100,000, and person B's by £10,000, then the difference in wealth expressed as a ratio will fall from 100:1 to 55:1, and this would *reduce* most measures of wealth inequality. But for person B to increase their wealth from £20,000 to £1,100,000 would now take almost 43 years of saving their entire income. This is a better way of thinking about what has been happening to wealth in the UK since (at least) the early 1990s: relative measures of wealth inequality may (or may not) have fallen slightly (from a high point), as wealth begins to spread down from the very top towards the middle of the distribution, but the gap between the haves and the have-a-lot-lesses is becoming ever harder for normal people to cross.

Why has wealth inequality changed over time?

As I discussed in Chapter 2, the long-term fall in both wealth inequality and the importance of wealth following the Second World War is attributed to high levels of tax on capital and income from capital, and fast-growing economies. Both phenomena persisted until the 1970s.

The rise in the importance of wealth since the 1970s is closely linked to housing wealth. The World Inequality Database's estimates are that housing made up 11% of total wealth of the wealthiest 1% in the UK in 1971, but 32% by 2012 (the equivalent figures for the wealthiest 10% are 22% in 1971 and 45% in 2012).[87] Much of this appears to be due to capital gains (i.e. the fact that houses have become more valuable) rather than because UK households have been prudently paying off their mortgages faster than they used to.[88] The impact of housing on measures of wealth *inequality* is a little unclear, though. Through the 1990s and 2000s, John Hills and colleagues estimate that the rise in the amount of property wealth *reduced* wealth inequalities. Now, it might seem wrong that increased property wealth reduces wealth inequality: surely, you might think, a house price boom is good news if you own a house, but terrible news if you do not, and so makes the gap between the home-owners and tenants even larger? Well, this is correct, but it turns out that a house price boom is not especially relevant for those at the very top of the wealth distribution, who tend to own most of their wealth outside of property (see Figure 3.10). Higher property prices and greater home ownership, instead, help the mid-wealthy to catch up with the super-wealthy (which reduces inequality), but increases the gap between those with no wealth and those in the middle (which increases inequality). As it happens, the former has been having a greater impact on the Gini coefficient. Conversely, estimates from the WAS suggest that, since the mid-2000s, property wealth has become more *unequally* distributed, because the proportion of households that own their own property has been falling, and so we have seen the opposite of what I describe above. But we know from the WAS that private pension wealth has become more widespread in recent years, and so less unequally distributed, and the combination of these two offsetting forces has left wealth inequality broadly unchanged since about 2000.[89]

Are inheritances contributing to greater inequality?

I summarised Thomas Piketty's predictions in Chapter 2. Unless societies respond in some way, he argues, some developed countries could end up resembling the Gilded Age, or la Belle Epoque, where the very rich are dominated by those who have inherited and then live off their wealth. 'Once constituted,' he argues, 'capital reproduces itself faster than output increases. The past devours the future.' But is Piketty's story consistent with UK data? We can break down his prediction into four parts:

1. Wealth is becoming more unequally distributed.
2. Wealth is growing in importance.
3. Much of the wealth that is accumulated is now being bequeathed, rather than spent.
4. Wealth is bequeathed to those who tend to be rich already.

I showed trends in inequality of wealth in the UK earlier in this chapter: the Gini coefficient for wealth in the UK (or the fraction of wealth held by the wealthiest 10%) is certainly very high compared with income, and is probably now a little higher its estimated low (i.e. most equally distributed) point in the 1970s.

Second, it is clear that wealth has been growing in importance in the UK in recent decades: the stock of household wealth was about 2 to 3 times as large as national income from 1950 to 1980, but at the turn of this decade stood at between 5½ to 6½ times the size of national income (depending on the data source), and was more than 6 times national income by 2014–16 according to the Wealth and Assets Survey (and, if Piketty and others are correct about the WAS missing out on the super-wealthy, then this will be an underestimate).[90] As I discussed earlier, an increasing amount of wealth even with unchanging inequality means that the wealthiest are, for all practical purposes, accelerating away from the rest of society.

The third part of Piketty's prediction is that much of the wealth that is accumulated is being bequeathed, rather than spent. Inheritances in the UK are certainly growing in importance: over the past few decades, the value of bequests has risen in real terms; more of us expect to bequeath something; and more of us have inherited, or expect to be able to inherit, something (75% of those born in the 1970s already have inherited or expect to inherit in the future, but just over a third of those born in the 1930s have inherited anything).[91] But because we have had good data on inheritances and wealth only since the mid-2000s, it is not yet clear whether inheritances are rising as a fraction of all wealth holdings, as Piketty predicted. (Piketty estimates that the value of all bequests and gifts as a fraction of

UK national income reached a low point in the 1970–90 period, and has been rising since.)[92] Hills and colleagues agree that the total size of estates as a fraction of national income has been rising since the 1980s. But this is the same pattern as I showed for total household wealth as a share of national income above; it does not necessarily mean that the fraction of wealth that is inherited, rather than accumulated in one's own lifetime, has been rising. So this point is not yet proven.

The final step in the puzzle is in determining whether inheritances are increasing inequalities. On the face of it, it is hard to see that inheritances can be doing anything to make us a more equal society. First, bequests themselves are very unequal: 85% of all wealth held by those aged 80 or over is held by half the population, with the other half having just 15%.[93] We know that the chances of receiving an inheritance peak for adults aged 55 to 64,[94] and are higher for those who have higher levels of education.[95] Those who already have wealth, or who have high lifetime incomes, are more likely to inherit and tend to inherit large sums than those who started off with less; similarly, people's perception of whether they are likely to receive an inheritance rises with income.[96] And there is also a pattern within couples: the likelihood that I receive an inheritance is higher if my partner has received one, another way that marriage and family formation exaggerate and perpetuate inequalities.[97]

Wealth can also pass between generations through transfers or gifts made when parents are alive. We think their total size is about a 10th that of inheritances. What little we know suggest that gifts are more likely to be made by those who have more wealth, but that being a well-off child reduces the likelihood of receiving a gift from your parents. So, although gifts are another way in which accumulated wealth can be transmitted through generations, one interpretation of the data is that parents might be doing their own form of within-family redistribution when they give out these gifts.[98]

However, some researchers have suggested that inheritances may have reduced – albeit very slightly – measures of wealth inequalities.[99] This is because some inheritances are received by those who otherwise would have very low levels of wealth and this does more to reduce a measure of wealth inequality like the Gini than does the fact that the wealthy are more likely to inherit, and more likely to inherit a lot. The same is true if we look at what inheritances do to someone's lifetime income. But others have argued that, if we take into account that all adults in the UK have some notional wealth in the form of their future state pension payments, then these modest inheritances actually make little difference to people's future standard of living, so inheritances have not been equalising the distribution of wealth.[100]

But as I discussed earlier, because our measures of inequality are relative, then the Gini coefficient can fall even though the gaps between the haves and have-nots seem as large as before. For example, and reusing the numbers from earlier in this chapter, if person A had £1,000,000 of wealth and then inherited £100,000 (a 10% rise in their wealth), and person B had £10,000 and inherited £10,000 (a 100% rise in their wealth), then typical measures of wealth inequality will fall. But if you assume that each person needs £25,000 a year to live on, then person A has gone from having enough wealth to last for 40 years to 44 years, and person B has gone from having enough wealth to last for $12 \times 2/5$ months to $12 \times 4/5$ months: if we measure 'for how long could this person live off their wealth?', then the gap has increased, not narrowed. The Resolution Foundation estimate that nearly half (46%) of non-home-owning 20–35 year olds have parents who do not own property either, but 83% of Millennial home-owners have a parent who also owns their own home.[101] This underlines that, whatever inheritances end up doing to summary measures of inequality, we can hardly expect the transfer of wealth between generations to reduce underlying inequalities in any meaningful sense. Overall, I conclude that, for all practical purposes, inheritances in the UK are currently widening the gap between those with a lot and a little of wealth, or those with low and high lifetime incomes. It seems to be a natural and benevolent activity to want to accumulate wealth and use that to provide for your children. The danger, though, as Heather Boushey's brilliant metaphor has it: '[a]s incomes accumulate into capital and then calcify into inheritances, the wealth of the dead takes on greater importance than that of the living'.[102] I return to this in the next chapter.

Conclusion

Piketty's alarming predictions (or warnings) cannot yet all be seen in the UK data on wealth holdings and inequality. But wealth is growing in importance, and remains very unequally distributed. Although we cannot yet see evidence of bequests leading to a class of trust-fund millionaires, the evidence I discussed in Chapter 2 on how inequality reduces social mobility provides an alternative explanation for how the children of the rich and wealthy grow up to be the same.

This chapter has explored trends in economic inequality in the UK, and some of the reasons for those trends. The UK saw a very large rise in income inequality in the 1980s that can be attributed mostly to a rise in inequality in what workers are paid, and to policy decisions to reduce top rates of tax and to increase social security benefits only in line with inflation, not earnings growth. Wages continued to grow more unequal through the 1990s, but other factors acted to prevent inequality from rising further. Data on top incomes tells a slightly different story, though, with the share of national income going to the top 1% or 0.1% continuing to rise until the onset of the financial crisis, and there is a suggestion that the main statistics on inequality are not capturing accurately the incomes of the richest. This is worrying, given that the fraction of national income going to the richest 0.01% (about 5,300 adults) has almost regained its historical high point. Wealth is considerably more unequally distributed in the UK than is income, with the wealthiest 10% owning between 44% and 52% (depending whose estimate we use) of all household wealth.

What can we say about where we are headed? I find it hard to be optimistic here. At the time of writing, UK government policy was to continue cutting spending on social security benefits through to 2020, and this will increase inequality. The state of the labour market over the next 3 to 10 years will depend heavily on the nature of the UK's future trading relationship with the rest of Europe (uncertain at the time of writing in early 2019), how the financial markets and the real economy adjust to any changes, and what policy changes governments choose to respond with. But any real growth in earnings will tend to widen slightly the distribution of income, because those in the top half of the distribution get more of their income from earnings than those at the bottom. More fundamentally, there is no sign of the pressures for increased wage inequality going away. It looks like top incomes fell back slightly in 2016–17, but earnings grew faster in 2017 at the top than anywhere else, and top earnings really accelerated away again in 2018 and 2019; when these changes show up in our data on top incomes, we could easily see record shares of income going to the richest 1% and 0.1%.[103]

In Chapter 2, I presented the evidence that high levels of inequality reduce social mobility and perpetuate divisions. Piketty's prediction of the emergence of a super-wealthy class of inheritors is not (yet) apparent in the UK, but household wealth is growing rapidly in importance and there is no sense in which the gap between the haves and the have-nots is shrinking. This means that, looking further ahead, the UK is likely to be suffering the hangover from its currently high levels of inequality for decades more.

But predictions about social science are not like the weather forecast. None of the phenomena I have discussed are due to an inexorable law of economics. All can be influenced or reversed, by us as consumers, workers and voters, as I suggest in the next chapter.

what should we do about inequality?

In Chapter 2, I presented research that argues that high levels of inequality are bad for us all. This suggests – although it is not all proven – that inequalities make our societies more stressful, less trusting and less pleasant, and act as a drag on economic growth. As inequalities grow, so the chance of getting ahead depends more on who you know and how much money you have, rather than your talents and skills. Left to their own devices, it seems that inequalities perpetuate, reinforcing the divisions between the haves and the have-nots. And in Chapter 3, I showed that the UK is near the top of the international league table for income inequality, that wealth is highly unequally distributed and growing in importance, and that the share of income going to the very rich is almost back at its historical high point. But the fact that inequality varies so much between similarly well-off countries tells us that what we see in the UK is not evitable.

With these in mind, what follows is a set of policy suggestions, many of which have been made before, to move the UK closer to a fairer, more productive and more pleasant society. They fall into six areas:

1. Towards a fairer labour market

2. Curbing excessive pay at the top

3. Redistributing wealth and inheritances

4. Providing security and opportunity for all

5. Promoting social mobility

6. Publishing better analysis about the state of economic inequalities in the UK

The first four will directly reduce the economic inequalities that I showed in Chapter 3. The fifth will move us closer to a level playing field for the next generation, offsetting some of the damaging aspects of inequality that I showed in Chapter 2. The final proposal reflects both that the data most used on inequality in the UK misses out on the experience of the very rich, and the huge importance that home-ownership has in determining the gaps between the well off and the not so well off.

These policy suggestions are not the final word. There is no single lever that governments need to pull to move us off a high inequality path. As Tony Atkinson said:

> Inequality is embedded in our social and economic structure, and a significant reduction requires us to examine all aspects of our society.[104]

He suggested, for example, that many areas of economic policy and most aspects of public services should have explicit anti-inequality or pro-poor biases. This is not what the economics in textbooks always teaches us, but Atkinson argues that '[t]here are distinct limits to what can be achieved by second-best taxes and transfers and, if we wish to make a significant reduction in inequality, there has to be recourse to a whole range of measures that have a – less than perfectly targeted – equalising impact'. Joseph Stiglitz argues forcibly that the financial sector is under-regulated and overly subsidised, and he argues that reforms to curb risk-taking, increase transparency and reduce offshore banking will be good for our economy and will help in the fight against inequality.

Stiglitz also argues passionately that the democratic and political systems in the United States urgently need reform to reduce the influence of the rich, and of corporations. If the political system or the media is one way in which inequalities and divisions perpetuate and the rich make life easier for themselves and harder for those that want to join them, then we in the UK must also do what we can to make money count for less in these spheres, although this is outside the scope of this book.[105]

Towards a fairer labour market

As most people in the UK get most of their income from their work (see Figure 1.3), and there are still large inequalities in earnings (see Figure 3.3), then reducing inequalities in pay is an obvious place to start.

I discussed earlier that the rise in earnings inequality since the 1980s was caused by skill-biased technological change and globalisation, and a fall in the importance and power of trade unions that was particularly marked in the UK. Wishing globalisation away, or trying to prevent labour-saving technological developments, is futile, and almost certainly counter-productive. In the long run, technological progress, including the growth of AI and the use of robots, will be beneficial, and if we can train (for example) more software engineers and data scientists, as well as – crucially – helping those whose jobs disappear develop new skills and find new ones – then it need not increase inequality. Both Atkinson suggested that governments should take a role in steering technological innovations; there is no reason why technological change need always be for the benefit of the highly skilled.[106] But it is a pervasive aspect of the labour market that those with skills that are not valued highly have little power, and those at the top have much more power (why are, say, careworkers forced to accept zero-hours contracts, or jobs that illegally pay them below the minimum wage by ignoring their time between their appointments, but this never happens to university professors?) But we can reduce that imbalance in power, to strengthen the ability of all workers to negotiate themselves a better deal from their employers.

A labour market strategy to reduce inequality would:

1. clamp down on exploitative employment practices, by redefining the boundary between self-employment and employment, and putting limits on the use of zero-hours contracts;

2. make it easier for workers to exercise their employment rights, by, for example, increasing enforcement of the minimum wage;

3. encourage collective bargaining or collective ownership;

4. keep the minimum wage rising broadly in line with wages in the rest of the economy;

5. invest in skills to help ensure that the gains from technological progress are shared equally.

In advocating these policies, I am fully embracing the idea that the economists' textbook concept of a market for labour has its limits, and is often an unhelpful guide to the correct policy response. Of course, wages are influenced by supply and demand – in the market for labour, 'supply' means how many workers can do and want to a certain job, and 'demand' means how badly do firms want to hire them – but it is wrong to think that there is some form of impersonal market in which wages are *determined* by supply and demand. Instead, there are uncertainties and complications everywhere. Firms might not know how badly they need someone in a particular role, and they will have little idea how good any particular candidate is. Workers know in principle that other jobs are available, but it takes time and money to find a job, and in the meantime bills need to be paid. Supply and demand put limits on the final wage that will be agreed, but there is scope for many things to affect the final outcome, including the strength of the firm's and worker's bargaining position, but also social norms, and notions of fairness and reputation. So, it should be possible to shift some employers off a low-pay, low-skill, high-turnover model without their going bust. For example, if we can get firms to concentrate more on the long run, then they should place more importance on getting a reputation for being a fair and generous employer, and start to care more about retaining and promoting staff so as not to lose expertise. Multiple equilibria, to use the economists' jargon, are possible.

One current concern in the UK is the rise in insecure or non-standard employment, or in so-called 'flexible' employment contracts where the flexibility benefits only the employer. The most obvious case of these is a zero-hours contract, but I am also including here so-called forced self-employment (where workers who might usually be hired as employees of a firm – which would give them access to sick pay, holiday pay, maternity rights and protection against unfair dismissal or exploitation – are made to be self-employed contractors selling their services to the firm). At the time of writing, the UK is debating whether to clamp down on some of these practices.[107] The tone of the debate is very similar to the one held over 20 years ago about whether the UK should introduce a national minimum wage. Back then, the main argument for a minimum wage was that some firms were taking advantage of workers who had little power and paying very low, exploitative, wages. On the other hand, some said that a minimum wage would destroy jobs, because jobs paying very low wages would not be profitable for firms if they had to pay more. Well, it turns out the doomsayers were wrong. When forced to pay higher wages, employers did so. There were hardly any job losses, and no overall fall in profits. Instead, firms coped: they absorbed the small increase in their wage bill, or they changed the way they used their workers.[108] The National Minimum Wage is now regarded as a great success; we need to remember all this when some employers tell us now that they need the flexibility of zero-hours contracts, or denying their workers their rights, in order to survive.

More generally, any change that meant that firms became a little more focused on the long run, and saw their employees as assets (and as fellow citizens) rather than a cost to be minimised, would help. A greater use of cooperatives, or other forms of employee-owned businesses, would help address power imbalances and reduce inequality, but it is difficult to know precisely what the government needs do to make these more likely (there is a risk that schemes to incentivise employers into making their employees into shareholders end up just helping better-off workers avoid income tax). Changes which lead to greater use of collective bargaining, or a greater role for trade unions, would certainly be welcome. Tony Atkinson suggested that the UK needs more bodies where employers, worker representatives and experts sit down collectively with government to discuss matters to do with the industrial strategy or the labour market. And some have argued that tackling climate change is going to require an entire overhaul of our tax system so that we tax heavily the use of natural resources or of polluting activities, and in return cut the taxes that firms have to pay when they employ people.

Minimum wages are the most direct way that the government can affect inequalities in the labour market, and I showed earlier that hourly wage inequality started to decline in the UK shortly after the first National Minimum Wage in 1999. At the moment, the levels of the minimum wage are set each year by the government, on the basis of advice from the Low Pay Commission (although the Low Pay Commission has been asked to ensure that the level of the minimum wage for those aged 25 or over reaches 60% of median wages by 2020). The Commission has tended to take a pragmatic and cautious approach to increases, but the downside is that employers have little idea of what the minimum wage might be in the future. Committing to having the minimum wage at least keep pace with wages elsewhere would give employers an additional encouragement to move away from a low-wage business model.

Dealing with excesses at the top

I explained earlier that the rising super-pay of top executives in the UK has a number of causes. First, it is difficult for firms to work out accurately just how much they need a particular executive, and it is very hard for them also to know how talented any top executive actually is. Second, there is an imbalance in power, but in this case the power seems to lie with the top executives, rather than with the ultimate owners of the firm, the shareholders. The outcome of this is very high remuneration deals which collectively, because of the way they underline divisions and distort the behaviour of those at the top, end up causing the rest of us harm.

Dealing with this problem will require action on two fronts:

1. Make changes to corporate governance so that the oversight of pay deals involves more of the company's stakeholders, and change company reporting rules to make the process of awarding top pay more transparent.

2. Increase, perhaps significantly, top rates of income tax, alongside tax reforms that make it harder to avoid tax.

The hope behind the first set of changes is that making pay arrangements more transparent or democratic will increase pressure on companies and senior managers to tone down their excesses. This could happen by requiring employee representative on remuneration committees; forcing companies to publish remuneration details of all those paid above a certain threshold (and not just the formal directors); giving shareholders more rights in voting on remuneration packages; and requiring companies to have a publicly accessible fair-pay policy; or a strategy to promote more active shareholders.[109] There is evidence that top executive pay is lower, on average, where there are more external board members (i.e. more supposedly impartial people overseeing remuneration), and that pay is both lower and more responsive to the executive's own performance where there are large institutional investors (like pension funds) holding shares in the company.[110] It is hard to see how any of my suggestions would cripple corporate performance or be an unreasonable encroachment on the freedom of top managers or executives. Why not try some, and see what happens?

A substantial rise in top rates of tax would be a reform of a very different character. To focus the mind, let us consider the recommendations made by economists Thomas Piketty and Tony Atkinson, and echoed recently by US Congresswoman Alexandria Ocasio-Cortez, that the highest rate of income tax be 65% or more, rather than the 45% it is in the UK at present. Perhaps this would apply only to incomes above £600,000 (in which case it would probably affect the richest 50,000 people or so, and only apply to income above that threshold) or perhaps even to incomes above £2.5 million (in which case it would probably affect only the richest 5,000 or so).

This new, much higher, rate of income tax will help in one of two ways. Either it will lead to extra tax revenues for governments to spend (or to recycle into tax cuts elsewhere), or it will significantly reduce the number of very high pay deals. Crucially, those advocating these sorts of tax rises would not mind if they did not lead to additional tax revenue for the Treasury. This is a very different situation from the debate in the UK some years ago when the Labour government of 2005–10 raised the top rate of tax from 40% to 50%, and the Coalition government of 2010–15 cut it back to 45% on the grounds that it was failing to bring in any more revenue for the UK Treasury.[111] Instead, the role of any new very high rate of income tax would be to reinforce that there are social costs to very high pay packets; it would be in part what economists call a *'Pigouvian tax'*, intended to discourage very high pay awards, just as most countries levy extra taxes on tobacco or fuel used for motoring because they harm others.

Other than reducing very high pay deals, or sucking it up and paying the additional income tax, there are several ways that companies and senior executives might react to a new 65% tax rate. First, companies might find ways to reward or encourage good performance other than remuneration (perhaps through swankier offices, or an exclusive lift). Now, these are classic examples of Veblen's conspicuous consumption, and so might worsen social anxieties; on the other hand, these things cannot be bequeathed, invested or used to give future generations a head-start. The second type of response would be for firms or executives to find ways to avoid income tax by structuring differently the way in which executives are paid. This would be bad, and a government wanting to introduce a new very high rate of tax would need also to clamp down on tax avoidance. A final threat is that multinational firms will move their very well-paid executives out of a country with a high rate of tax to a lower-tax country, and then the high-taxing country will miss out on the tax revenues on all of the executives' salary. This is a risk, and it is an excellent argument in favour of international discussion and cooperation on tax matters. But it might be an idle threat: the tax rate on earnings above £150,000 a year used to be 40% in the late 1990s, and now it's 47%, but the income share of the top 1% is still rising. 'Global financial elites are more likely to die than to move to a different country', say Lee Elliot Major and Stephen Machin, reviewing research by sociologist Cristobal Young and colleagues.[112]

Wealth and inheritance

I showed in Chapter 3 the extent of wealth inequality in the UK (high), the importance of wealth (growing) and Piketty's prediction for what will happen during the twenty-first century (a return to the levels of inequality at the turn of the twentieth century).

To prevent this, action will be needed on two fronts:

1. Change the way that property, financial wealth and inheritances are taxed.

2. Introduce policies to promote savings and to give young people a capital endowment.

In the UK, property, pensions and inheritances are all under-taxed.[113] Removing these unjustified tax breaks would slow down the growth in wealth inequality, as well as contribute additional tax revenue to the Treasury. For example, to tax property wealth fairly, council tax bills should rise in line with property values (so that, say, the tax on a property worth £2 million would be 10 times as large as one worth £200,000; at present, the bills for the most expensive houses are, at most, three times as large as those for the cheapest houses in the same area),[114] and some of the exemptions from capital gains tax that apply to domestic homes should be reviewed. In the longer term, it would be sensible to have a 'housing services tax' that is charged to everyone who owns a property and that would depend, broadly, on its value, similar to the system of domestic rates that operated before 1990.

We also under-tax pension saving: there is little point providing a tax incentive to save in a pension over and above other forms of saving. A sensible reform would remove the ability to take out a lump sum free of tax upon retirement, and by taxing properly the contribution that employers make to pension pots. Currently, most of the money currently spent on these unneeded tax breaks simply goes to help the well off.

It may be that the only things one cannot escape are death and taxes, but, in the UK, dying is lot more tax privileged than it needs to be. Inheritance tax – which is paid on the value of estates above £325,000, but with many exceptions – is relatively easy to avoid (only 4% of estates were liable to it in 2015–16)[115] and there are other tax breaks that apply on death which do not need to be there. In the short run, some of the tax breaks that apply at death should be scrapped. But it is not the fact that people bequeath money when they die that makes inequalities worse: it is the fact that too much of these inheritances go to too few people, and that many of those that inherit were well off to begin with. To address that directly, an ambitious reform would replace inheritance tax with a tax that depends on the value of the inheritances that individuals receive over their lifetime (perhaps allowing for an initial amount free of any tax, say £50,000).[116] This would allow bequests to be left free of tax, but it would help reduce the concentration of very high levels of wealth among a few.

None of these proposals would unfairly penalise those with wealth. Instead, they correct anomalies in the current UK tax system that unjustifiably favour certain types of wealth, or certain ways of saving, over others. To go further in tackling the problems of wealth inequality, some have recommended an explicit wealth tax, where everyone pays each year a fraction of their stock of net wealth, structured so that the wealthy pay a higher rate than the less wealthy. This is the main recommendation of Thomas Piketty's book, and it his solution for reversing the $r > g$ relationship that he suggests will be so damaging to future societies. If the UK were to implement a wealth tax, then some of the financial wealth in this country might quickly flee to countries not operating such a tax. But that does not mean that such a tax should not be attempted.

The second group of policies would tackle wealth inequalities by boosting the wealth owned by those who have very little. There are several

ways this could be done. One idea is to give all citizens a capital endowment, perhaps when they reach the age of 18. To be effective at reducing
wealth inequalities, the endowment would need to be large – tens of thousands of pounds, rather than hundreds of pounds – and so some who
advocate this also want to see reforms to inheritance tax, like those mentioned above, so that the extra tax revenues collected from inheritances or
bequests can be recycled into a wealth handout for all. This is a politically
appealing link to make, but there is no need to limit the generosity of these
endowments to the tax revenues that come from inheritances.

A related idea is to subsidise savings made by those on low incomes
so that they can be encouraged (and supported) in building up their own
financial wealth. One idea is to have a state-run savings institution that
guarantees all savers a rate of interest that is greater than the rate of
inflation on a certain amount of their savings.[117] Another would be a
scheme where the government actively tops up, or match funds, savings
made by low-income households (up to a certain level).[118]

Providing security and opportunity to all

This set of policy suggestions also reduces inequalities of outcomes
directly by helping those towards the bottom of the income distribution.
But it is very difficult to achieve equality of opportunity in the future without some reducing inequalities in outcomes now. What those who have
money and wealth often fail to appreciate is that, irrespective of whether it
brings you health and happiness, affluence definitely provides security and
power, and this has important implications for future levels of inequality.
When people's positions are secure, then they can take greater risks, and
they can cope better with temporary setbacks. But if you have too little
income, or no wealth, then you face chronic insecurity. Compared with the
secure individual, you will spend more of your resources simply surviving,
and you will be more vulnerable to unexpected shocks to your job, health
or family (and this is on top of any differences in prices faced by those on
low incomes, the so-called 'poverty premium'[119]). In the long run, there is
a pay-off to this increased security, and this is another way in which the
gaps in society get bigger.

There are powerful moral or human rights arguments in favour of
universalism – or that our governments should provide for all of us. But
here I am making a practical, evidence-based argument that, to combat

inequality, we have to ensure decent minimum standards for all by doing what we can with our public services and the welfare state to provide a sense of security, or a safety net when things go wrong. So an anti-inequality strategy should include the following:

- A comprehensive social security system that protects us (and especially our children) against a lack of suitable jobs, ill-health, disability or family breakdown, and does so in a way that promotes dignity. These social security benefits need to be uprated by more than price inflation so that those dependent on them do not fall further behind the rest of society.

- An economic policy that promotes full employment (or the reduction of involuntary unemployment or under-employment), for men and women, in a way that is consistent with providing support to those when there are no suitable jobs and respects our need to balance work and family life.

- A comprehensive welfare state that provides access to health services, education and training for children and adults, and recourse to the legal system to enforce one's rights. This may well mean reversing some of the cuts to public services imposed since 2010.

Some have advocated a basic income system to reduce inequality, or as a response to the changing nature of the world of work and the rise of insecure employment. There are powerful philosophical arguments for a basic income, and in some countries the welfare state is so under-developed that it makes political sense to argue for a universal basic income scheme. But I think the argument that the UK needs a basic income scheme as a way to counter economic inequality and promote equality of opportunity is less strong than in some other countries. At the time of writing, the UK is mid-way through a seemingly never-ending process of introducing Universal Credit, and there are certainly many flaws with both Universal Credit and the previous mishmash of benefits and tax credits. But the principle behind the social security system in the UK is that, if your resources are too low, then the state will give you more, provided you also do your bit to help yourself. Sure, we do not have a fully *individualised, unconditional* social security system, and some who argue for a basic income scheme think that it should be paid to each adult, regardless of how well off they or their household is, or whether they make any effort to look for work. But nor does the UK have a system that systematically excludes certain groups from receiving support. The political difficulty of a universal basic income system in the UK is that it would require very large tax rises to allow governments to afford to pay a basic income to the rich as well as continuing to support those at the bottom currently receiving social security benefits.[120] But some of the benefits of a basic income might be achieved by reforming our current set of benefits, perhaps removing some of the conditions (if that is what is required), or by making them more generous (if that is the goal), or in ways that encourage take-up and promote dignity.

Social mobility and education

The policy suggestions in the four areas above would directly reduce economic inequalities. The main idea in this section is to help offset the harmful ways that high levels of inequality hold back social mobility. Tackling this will require:

1. getting serious about social mobility being one of government's, and society's, key goals;

2. promoting equality of opportunity in the education system.

All political parties in the UK say they strongly support social mobility; indeed, it would be tough for anyone to argue that we should not have equality of opportunity. As Lee Elliot Major and Stephen Machin say, 'prime ministers come and go, but all seem to return to the damning [findings that social mobility in the UK is declining] as they outline their hopes for a more mobile society'.[121] And in the last couple of decades, the UK has had strategies, and commissions, and probably task forces too, to go alongside these hopes. What we have had rather fewer of is what ultimately matters: policies, and improved outcomes; this might explain why all of the Social Mobility Commissioners resigned in 2017 because of a perceived lack of support from government.[122]

Having commissions in itself is not a bad idea – and I am about to recommend another one. There is no one single change that needs to be made to improve social mobility: it requires a coordinated focus, and a change in culture across local and national government. Left to their own devices, government departments can forget that this is a goal worth striving for; inevitably, all the costs of improving social mobility are incurred now, and the pay-off will be decades in the future. So, a government that is serious about social mobility should set up an independent Social Mobility Commission to produce a regular, independent, assessment of what extent the UK does have equality of opportunity. The Commission needs to have the political clout to make policy recommendations across all areas of government – perhaps by having it report to Parliament and not to the government of the day. And either the Commission should have the resources to assess all policy proposals against what they do to promote or hinder equality of opportunity, or government departments should be obliged to do this themselves (similarly, local authorities could be asked to produce their own reports setting out what they do to promote or hinder equality of opportunity).

But there is plenty to do while we wait for such a Commission to report, and we should start with our education system. As Lee Elliot Major and Stephen Machin say, 'far from acting as the great social leveller, education has been commandeered by the middle classes to retain their advantage from one generation to the next. Our social elites will go to ever great lengths to ensure their offspring stay ahead.'[123] The Sutton Trust, a charity devoted to promoting social mobility through education, released a Mobility Manifesto in 2017, with a set of recommendations that respond directly to the evidence that I set out in Chapter 2 about what it is that well-off parents do to pass on their advantaged situation to their children; it is a great place for any politician to start.[124] Achieving social mobility through education will mean giving opportunities to all children, both in the early years and post-18, whether they are at grammar schools or comprehensives, whether they are academically gifted and want to go to university, or want vocation training and work-based apprenticeships.

But measures like these are only tinkering. A huge flaw with the system of publicly funded education in England is the way that better-off families can buy their way into certain state-run schools through the housing market. This is school selection by mortgage, and it 'reinforces school segregation and inequalities in performance and achievement, and reduces social mobility across the generations'.[125] Probably the only fair solution is to make more use of lotteries to determine admission to state-run schools, rather than criteria related to distance from school or living in a catchment area. Here, though, emotions run high, and reform is difficult because it is close to a zero-sum game. If a lottery means that one child is able to attend a desirable school that they would not normally be able to attend, then another child whose parents have strategically 'invested' in living in that catchment area will lose out. At the same time, it would be worth changing the law so that private schools are not able to benefit from charitable status.

Parents cannot buy their children's way into university as directly as they can with schools, but a lot about applying to universities in the UK tilts the process in favour of the advantaged, including the use of predicted grades, the importance attached to personal statements on application forms, and in-person interviews (and this is before considering that advantaged children are more likely to be at better schools that achieve higher grades and have a track record in putting forward candidates to good universities). Universities do valuable outreach work to try and persuade those young people who know little about universities to apply; this should continue. But just as lotteries for school places are proposed as the only way for school choice to be fair, so a fair, social-mobility-promoting system of university entry would have each university specify its minimum entrance criteria, allow young people to apply, and then allocate places by a lottery if courses are over-subscribed. As Elliot Major and Machin conclude, 'improving relative social mobility is never going to be easy. Powerful but pragmatic measures are needed to smash through glass floors and glass ceilings. Randomly allocating equally deserving candidates to over-subscribed schools and universities is the only way of levelling the education playing field.'[126]

Finally, we should do what we can to our system of education and training after school so that all young people receive opportunities to acquire further skills, and that we subsidise these opportunities such as we support those who go on to university.

Publishing better analysis about the state of economic inequalities in the UK

The appendix found at **mikebrewereconomics.com/WDWK** discusses the advantages and limitations of different ways of measuring inequality, and the different sources of data on economic inequality in the UK.

The final suite of proposals would improve the quality of the statistics on economic inequality in the UK. They are that:

1. official statistics on income inequality should include a variant where the concept of income includes the implicit rental income that accrues to home-owners, as discussed in the appendix at **mikebrewereco nomics.com/WDWK**;

2. more should be done to ensure that the situation of the very rich is reflected in debates about inequality. This could be done by improving the way that data from household surveys is corrected to account for the very rich, or by the ONS or similar publishing the data on top income shares alongside other inequality statistics.[127]

These might seem like technical, nerdy issues. But how we measure the state of our society is important, and changes in how facts are presented can easily affect the demand for policy action. For example, because houses tend to be owned by those who are richer or older, looking at a measure of income that includes implicit rental income is going to give us a different impression of the nature of income inequality in the UK. And most of the changes within the top 1% and especially the top 0.1% or 0.01% – who are continuing to grow richer and pull away from the rest of us – are missed by the main inequality statistics. As Thomas Piketty said: 'Those who have a lot of [money] never fail to defend their interests. Refusing to deal with numbers rarely serves the interests of the least well-off'.[128]

Conclusion

This chapter has suggested what we should do to move the UK off its high-inequality path. Few of the proposals are new. High levels of inequality persist not through a lack of ideas, but a lack of the political will or ability to make changes. And, in many cases, the precise detail of what we do is less important than the fact that we do something. But the ideas in this chapter would be an excellent place to start.

conclusion

In 2014, Mark Carney, an economist and Governor of the Bank of England, said that:

> Inclusive capitalism is fundamentally about delivering a basic social contract comprised of relative equality of outcomes; equality of opportunity; and fairness across generations.[129]

He noted that there was 'hard data' supporting the idea that 'this basic social contract is breaking down'. The sort of people appointed to run central banks are not renowned for being radical firebrands, so, if a usually mild-mannered central banker is concerned about inequality, then we should treat it as a serious political and economic issue.

My aim for this book was to set out what we know about, and what we should do about, the high levels of economic inequalities in the UK. Income inequality in the UK is one of the highest among comparable rich countries, second only to the United States among major economies, and beaten only by Lithuania elsewhere in Europe. But it has also become clear that the main data used to estimate the shape of the UK income distribution does a bad job at reflecting the circumstances of the very rich. With new analysis, I have shown that, although the very rich in the UK did get hit by the financial crisis, they have now recovered, and the fraction of national income going to the richest 0.01% (about 5,300 adults) has almost regained its historical high point. I also showed that wealth is even more unequally distributed in the UK than is income, with the wealthiest 10%

owning between 44% and 52% of all household wealth (depending on which estimate you believe). Household wealth is growing in importance (as Piketty highlighted) and, although the Gini coefficient for the wealth distribution may not be changing, there is no practical sense in which the gap between the haves and the have-nots is shrinking.

Mark Carney said that equality of opportunity and of outcomes were good for growth, good for our well-being and for promoting a sense of community, and reflected fundamental views about social justice. He could have gone further. What has changed in the past couple of decades has been a new wave of evidence on the damaging effects of inequality. We know now that countries with high levels of inequality have lower rates of growth, are more stressed and anxious, less happy and healthy, and have lower feelings of solidarity or trust across society. And there are good arguments, although not yet conclusive, that there is a cause and effect relationship from high inequality to a weaker, less prosperous society. If so, then the problem with high levels of inequality is not just that the rich capture so much that there is not enough to share round the rest of society now, but that there will be less to share round for everyone in the future. We have also learnt more in recent years about how inequalities perpetuate. Hard data and careful research show that the greater are inequalities of outcomes, the harder it is to achieve equality of opportunity and the less social mobility there will be, deepening divisions in society. And there is now a warning that, if we continue with our current economic and political policies, the twenty-first century will see the emergence of a super-wealthy elite, just as existed at the dawn of the twentieth century.

There is an argument that we in the UK should not be overly concerned about inequality, because it has been over 30 years since the UK saw a concerted rise in income inequality. Needless to say, this is not an argument I support. Every year of high inequality is another year that strains our sense of fairness and of social justice, and another year where equality of opportunity becomes harder to achieve. The UK is still one the most unequal of all rich, developed economies, and it does not need to be this way. Because of this, I have also set out what we should do to reduce inequality in the UK. My policy proposals would help make the labour market fairer, curb excessive remuneration at the top, redistribute wealth and inheritances, provide security and opportunity to all, and promote social mobility. I also think we need better informed analysis about the state of economic inequalities in the UK. Although I have not been able to assess quantitatively what impact these policies would have, I tried to think what would be needed to change the Gini for income or wealth by several percentage points (following Tony Atkinson's guidelines), or to undo the way that the education system entrenches, rather than breaks down, social inequalities.

These proposals might seem radical, naïve or politically infeasible. But I cannot imagine that inequality in the UK could be brought back down towards what is normal for a rich, modern, democratic country without action in the areas I set out. If my proposals for, say, tackling wealth inequalities or curbing supersonic pay deals strike you as too radical, by all means find alternatives that will achieve similar things. And what is and is not politically feasible is not fixed for all time: it is simply the collective view of society right now. Voters, politicians and other social actors can all play their part in shifting the boundaries of what policy responses are politically feasible, and what levels of inequality are socially acceptable. I hope this book has provided you with arguments and evidence to help achieve that.

notes

1. From the Foreword to Keeley (2015).
2. www.oxfam.org/en/even-it/5-shocking-facts-about-extreme-global-inequality-and-how-even-it-davos
3. Pooley (2019).
4. Address at Grandes Conferences Catholiques, Brussels, 17 June 2015.
5. See Dorling et al. (2016), for example.
6. Robinson (2019); Irwin (2019).
7. www.oecd.org/social/inequality.htm (accessed February 2019).
8. Manipulation of the post-tax figures in Tables 1 and 2 of Piketty et al. (2018).
9. See https://wid.world
10. At the time of writing, the latest government reports are DWP (2019). A slightly different data source is used for ONS (2019b).
11. See Jenkins (2011) for the UK, or Garnero et al. (2019) for international comparisons.
12. The latest data is analysed in Bourquin et al. (2019) and DWP (2019).
13. All facts in this book use the Modified OECD equivalence scale: see OECD (n.d.) or mikebrewereconomics.com/WDWK for more details.
14. See Brewer et al. (2017).
15. See also 'Thing 20' in Chang (2010), or Roemer and Trannoy (2016).
16. Blair (2005).
17. See Anand and Segal (2015), Lakner's chapter in Boushey et al. (2017), and Alvaredo et al. (2018).
18. Derived from Table 11 of ONS (2019b).
19. Giles (2018) is an example of this viewpoint.
20. See Dorling and Thomas (2016), for example.
21. See Willetts (2010) or The Intergenerational Commission (2018), for example.
22. Jenkins (2011) does, though, for example.
23. See Savage (2015) or Friedman and Laurison (2019), for example.
24. Rowlingson (2011) and Goldhammer's chapter in Boushey et al. (2017) contain guides to the initial debate in the UK and United States respectively.
25. Bergh et al. (2016).
26. Taken from Wilkinson and Pickett (2018); the phrase is from Rudyard Kipling's poem 'We and They'.

27. Marmot (2004).
28. See de Graaf et al. (2001) and James (2007).
29. Mijs (2019) shows that people in high-inequality countries are more likely to believe that unequal outcomes are based on merit, and not due to underlying structural barriers preventing equal outcomes.
30. Atkinson (2015: 305).
31. See Ostry et al. (2019). Some of the original works are Cingano (2014), Ostry et al. (2014) and Dabla-Norris et al. (2015).
32. Brueckner and Lederman (2015).
33. Figure 5 of Grigoli and Nobles (2017).
34. Figure 3 of Cingano (2014).
35. See Dabla-Norris et al. (2015), Morelli's chapter in Boushey et al. (2017) and Ostry et al. (2019). Madsen et al. (2018) shows that inequality reduces savings, investment, education and knowledge production, all important determinants of economic growth, across OECD countries.
36. Stiglitz (2012), with a summary in Stiglitz (2015).
37. United Nations (2009), commonly known as the Stiglitz Report.
38. Kumhof et al. (2015).
39. Ostry et al. (2019).
40. See Francis and Hutchings (2013) or Doepke and Zilibotti (2019).
41. This graph was named 'the Great Gatsby curve' by the late Alan Krueger, who at the time was Chair of the Council of Economic Advisers to President Obama, but I confess I had to look up the plot on Wikipedia when I first came across this term to understand the reference. He introduced the phrase in Krueger (2012), but he drew on research subsequently published in Corak (2013a, b).
42. See Jerrim and Macmillan (2015) and Doepke and Zilibotti (2019).
43. Chetty et al. (2017).
44. Stiglitz (2012: xlix).
45. See, for example, the edited volume by Boushey et al. (2017) with contributions from across economics, the Piketty Symposium (2014), which contains comments from sociologists, and Wealth and Inequality (2015), which contained an initial reaction from economists.
46. See Acemoglu and Robinson (2015) and DeLong et al.'s chapter in Boushey et al. (2017).
47. See Solow's chapter in Boushey et al. (2017), or Ray (2015). On the other hand, Madsen (2017), using data from the UK since 1210, finds that r and g 'are robust and significant determinants of wealth and income inequality, and have been the major forces behind the large inequality waves over the past eight centuries'.

48. See Piketty et al. (2018) and Smith et al. (2019) for two sides of the debate.
49. The first point has been made by many (see, for example, Acemoglu and Robinson, 2015). For the second, see Nielsen's chapter in Boushey et al. (2017).
50. Atkinson and Jenkins (2019).
51. See Bourquin et al. (2019) and DWP (2019).
52. See Jenkins (1995), Blundell and Etheridge (2010) and Blundell et al. (2018).
53. See Jenkins (1995) and Brewer and Wren-Lewis (2015).
54. See Brewer and Wren-Lewis (2015) and Belfield et al. (2017).
55. The rest of this subsection draws on Cribb et al. (2017) and Cribb et al. (2018).
56. Section 8 of ONS (2019a).
57. Machin (2011), Lindley and Machin (2013) or D'Arcy (2018) for more details on wage inequality in the UK.
58. Tanndal and Waldenström (2018).
59. OECD (2019).
60. Simms (2019).
61. Belfield et al. (2017) and Blundell et al. (2018).
62. Clark and Leicester (2004).
63. See Browne and Elming (2015) and De Agostini et al. (2018).
64. Norris Keiller and Waters (2018).
65. This work was first collected together in Atkinson and Piketty (2007), and is available at the World Inequality Database at https://wid.world
66. This section draws on Brewer and Sámano-Robles (2019).
67. Analysis of more recent Survey of Personal Incomes data is available at www.gov.uk/government/collections/personal-incomes-statistics, but this does not include top income shares or estimates of what income would be needed to be in the (say) top 1% of adults; all the analysis is done only for taxpayers.
68. As this book was being finalised, the Office for National Statistics released experimental estimates of what fraction of household disposable income goes to the richest 1% of individuals, and estimate this to be 7.1% in 2018. The main differences between that estimate and the one shown here are that the ONS uses disposable (so, after-tax) income, and income at the household level. See ONS (2019c).
69. Piketty (2014: 252).
70. Smith et al. (2019) show that much of the non-wage income at the top of the distribution in the United States is actually income from businesses that the wealthy people both own and work in, and so they argue that it should also be thought of as earned income, rather than representing the idle rich. It is not clear whether this also applies to the UK.

71. Förster et al. (2014) compares top income shares in OECD countries, but there is more up-to-date data at wid.world. The richest 1% take a greater share of national income in China and South Africa than they do in the UK.
72. Figure 5 of Burkhauser et al. (2018a) suggests that the survey data underestimates the true Gini by between 0.5 ppts to just under 3 ppts in the worst year. The 'correction' is discussed in Burkhauser et al. (2018b).
73. This is new analysis from the Survey of Personal Incomes (HMRC, 2018a), pooling data from 2013–14 to 2015–16. It includes analysis of the so-called 'composite' cases: see Brewer and Sámano-Robles (2019).
74. Bell and Van Reenan (2013, 2014).
75. Atkinson (2015: 89).
76. This phrase is from Robeyns (2016).
77. This leads to one of Piketty's best put-downs: 'Among the members of upper income groups are US academic economists, many of whom believe that the economy of the US is working fairly well and, in particular, that it rewards talent and merit accurately and precisely. This is a very comprehensible human reaction' (p.296).
78. See Edmans and Gabaix (2016).
79. See Tyson and Spence's chapter in Boushey et al. (2017).
80. See Piketty et al. (2014) and Rubolino and Waldenström (2017a, b).
81. ONS (2018a).
82. All from ONS (2018a).
83. Balestra and Tonkin (2018). Zucman (2019) compares wealth inequality over a very long period for those few countries where data is available, using data from https://wid.world
84. Alvaredo et al. (2016a).
85. Piketty's estimates were challenged by the journalist Chris Giles, and a summary of the dispute can be found in Reed (2014): it related mostly to whether one should prefer the data from estates or household surveys. It is not clear why Piketty's estimates are greater than those of his collaborators that can be found in the WID database, and which are discussed in Alvaredo et al. (2016b). An even newer estimate of wealth inequalities is in Cummins (2019).
86. As done in, for example, Gardiner (2017).
87. Table H.3 in Alvaredo et al. (2016b).
88. See Hills et al. (2013) and D'Arcy and Gardiner (2017). Madsen (2019) agrees, having looked over a much longer time period.
89. Table 4 in ONS (2018a).
90. Historical numbers are from Figure 2.4 in Hills et al. (2013) and Figure 3.1 in Piketty (2014).

91. Hood and Joyce (2017).
92. Figure 11.12 of Piketty (2014).
93. Hood and Joyce (2017).
94. Hills et al. (2013) and ONS (2018b).
95. Crawford and Hood (2015) and Hood and Joyce (2017).
96. Hood and Joyce (2017).
97. Crawford and Hood (2015).
98. Hills et al. (2013).
99. See Hills et al. (2013), Crawford and Hood (2015) and ONS (2018b).
100. Crawford and Hood (2015).
101. Gardiner (2017).
102. Boushey et al. (2017: 363).
103. HMRC (2019) suggests top incomes fell back slightly at the top in 2016–17, but Figure 11 of Resolution Foundation (2019) shows how earnings grew across the distribution in 2017 and 2018, with 2018 especially showing an inequality-increasing pattern; see also paragraph 4.25 of OBR (2019).
104. Atkinson (2015: 3).
105. Jones (2014) suggests ways in which the wealthy are able to exert power and influence over politics and policy in the UK.
106. Atkinson (2015: 118).
107. Recent proposals were published in Department for Business, Energy and Industrial Strategy (2018), but the TUC is still calling for an end to zero-hours contracts; see Collinson (2019).
108. See Plunkett and Hurrell (2013), especially Chapter 2 and references therein.
109. For example, see the recommendations in High Pay Commission (2011).
110. Bell and Van Reenen (2016).
111. HMRC (2012).
112. Elliot Major and Machin (2018), who cite Young et al. (2016) and Young (2017).
113. See Mirrlees et al. (2011) or Brewer and Kanabar (2016).
114. The limit of three times higher applies in England. It is 3.5 times in Wales, and 3.67 times in Scotland.
115. HMRC (2018b).
116. Atkinson (2015: 194).
117. Atkinson (2015: 168).
118. A scheme similar to this (and known as the Savings Gateway) was due to come into force in 2010, but was scrapped by the incoming Coalition government.
119. Corfe and Keohane (2018).
120. Goulden (2018).
121. Elliot Major and Machin (2018: 26).

122. Milburn (2017).
123. Elliot Major and Machin (2018: 11).
124. Sutton Trust (2017).
125. Elliot Major and Machin (2018: 90).
126. Elliot Major and Machin (2018: 210).
127. As this book was being finalised, the ONS announced an improvement to one of its series which partially, but by no means completely, addresses this: see ONS (2019c).
128. Piketty (2014: 577).
129. Carney (2014).

further reading and key data sources

A general reader looking to learn more about the arguments in Chapter 2 should start with the following works (listed in alphabetical order): Atkinson (2015), Boushey et al. (2017), Doepke and Zilibotti (2019), Elliot Major and Machin (2018), Ostry et al. (2019), Piketty (2014), Stiglitz (2012), Wilkinson and Pickett (2009, 2018).

Key data sources

Income inequality

There are two government publications with statistics on income inequality. One is known as 'Households Below Average Income', the latest of which at the time of finalising this book is DWP (2019), covering data up to 2017–18, although the analysis shown in this book uses the previous year's release. It and future releases can be found at: www.gov.uk/government/collections/households-below-average-income-hbai--2. The other is 'The effects of taxes and benefits on household income, disposable income estimate: 2018', the latest of which is ONS (2019b), and is available from: www.ons.gov.uk/peoplepopulationandcommunity/personalandhouse-holdfinances/incomeandwealth.

Each year, researchers at the Institute for Fiscal Studies produce a report on inequality and poverty, the latest of which are Bourquin et al. (2019) and Cribb et al. (2018). These, as well as useful statistics on the income distribution, can be downloaded from: www.ifs.org.uk/tools_and_resources/incomes_in_uk.

Estimates of income inequality for other countries can be downloaded from the OECD website (https://data.oecd.org/inequality/income-inequality.htm) or the World Inequality Database (https://wid.world/).

Analysis of the Survey of Personal Incomes is published by HM Revenue and Customs (www.gov.uk/government/collections/personal-incomes-statistics), but this does not include top income shares or estimates of what income would be needed to be in the top 1% (say) of adults; all of the HM Revenue and Customs analysis is done only for taxpayers. Until the recommendations in this book are taken up, the only source of data on top income shares for the UK is the World Inequality Database (https://wid.world/). Brewer and Sámano-Robles (2019) contains the data behind the new analysis on top incomes in the UK shown in Chapter 3.

Wealth inequality

The latest findings from the Office for National Statistics' 'Wealth and Assets Survey' are ONS (2018a), which is available from: www.ons.gov.uk/peoplepopulationandcommunity/personalandhouseholdfinances/incomeandwealth. Alternative data on top wealth shares, as produced by Alvaredo et al. (2016b), is available at the World Inequality Database (https://wid.world/).

Other

The data underpinning all figures in this book is available on request from the author, whose details can be found at **mikebrewereconomics.com/WDWK**.

references

Acemoglu, D. and Robinson, J. (2015) The Rise and Decline of General Laws of Capitalism. *Journal of Economic Perspectives, 29*(1), 3–28.

Alvaredo, F., Atkinson, A. and Morelli, S. (2016a) The Challenge of Measuring UK Wealth Inequality in the 2000s. *Fiscal Studies, 13*(1), 13–36.

Alvaredo, F., Atkinson, A. and Morelli, S. (2016b) Top Wealth Shares in the UK over more than a Century, WID.world WP 2017/2.

Alvaredo, F., Chancel, L., Piketty, T., Saez, E. and Zucman, G. (2018) *The World Inequality Report*, wir2018.wid.world

Anand, S. and Segal, P. (2015) The Global Distribution of Income. In A. Atkinson and T. Piketty (eds), *Handbook of Income Distribution Volume 2A*. Amsterdam: Elsevier.

Atkinson, A. (2015) *Inequality: What Can Be Done?* Cambridge, MA: Harvard University Press.

Atkinson, A. and Jenkins, S. (2019) A Different Perspective on the Evolution of UK Income Inequality. IZA Discussion Paper 11884.

Atkinson, A. and Piketty, T. (eds) (2007) *Top Incomes Over the Twentieth Century*. Oxford: Oxford University Press.

Balestra, C. and Tonkin, R. (2018) Inequalities in Household Wealth across OECD Countries: Evidence from the OECD Wealth Distribution Database. *OECD Statistics* Working Papers, 2018/01. Paris: OECD. doi: 10.1787/7e1bf673-en

Belfield, C., Blundell, R., Cribb, J., Hood, A. and Joyce, R. (2017) Two Decades of Income Inequality in Britain: The Role of Wages, Household Earnings and Redistribution. *Economica, 84*, 157–79.

Bell, B. and Van Reenen, J. (2013) Extreme Wage Inequality: Pay at the Very Top. *American Economic Review, 103*(3), 153–7.

Bell, B. and Van Reenen, J. (2014) Bankers and Their Bonuses. *Economic Journal, 124*, F1–21. doi: 10.1111/ecoj.12101

Bell, B. and Van Reenen, J. (2016) CEO Pay and the Rise of Relative Performance Contracts: A Question of Governance? NBER Working Paper No. 22407.

Bergh, A., Nilsson, T. and Waldenström, D. (2016) *Sick of Inequality?* Cheltenham: Edward Elgar.

Blair, T. (2005) We've Got To Carry This On. *Progress*, March, www.progressonline.org.uk/2005/03/21/weve-got-to-carry-this-on/

Blundell, R. and Etheridge, B. (2010) Consumption, Income and Earnings Inequality in Britain. *Review of Economic Dynamics, 13,* 76–102.

Blundell, R., Joyce, R., Norris Keiller, A. and Ziliak, J. (2018) Income Inequality and the Labour Market in Britain and the US. *Journal of Public Economics, 162,* 48–62.

Bourquin, P., Cribb, J., Norris Keiller, A. and Xu, X. (2019) In 2017–18, average household income growth stalled for first time since 2012–13, Institute for Fiscal Studies Briefing Note 245.

Boushey, H., Delong, J. B. and Steinbaum, M. (2017) *After Piketty: The Agenda for Economics and Inequality.* Cambridge, MA: Harvard University Press.

Brewer, M., Etheridge, B. and O'Dea, C. (2017) Why Are Households that Report the Lowest Incomes So Well-off? *Economic Journal, 127,* F24–49. doi: 10.1111/ecoj.12334

Brewer, M. and Kanabar, R. (2016) The role of the UK tax system in an anti-poverty strategy, University of Essex, www.iser.essex.ac.uk/files/iser_reports/reports/pdf/Anti_poverty_strategy_Brewer.pdf.

Brewer, M. and Sámano-Robles, C. (2019) Top incomes in the UK: Analysis of the 2015–16 Survey of Personal Incomes, forthcoming as Institute for Social and Economic Research Working Paper.

Brewer, M. and Wren-Lewis, L. (2015) Accounting for Changes in Income Inequality: Decomposition Analyses for the UK, 1978–2008. *Oxford Bulletin of Economics and Statistics,* doi: 10.1111/obes.12113

Browne, J. and Elming, W. (2015) The effect of the coalition's tax and benefit changes on household incomes and work incentives, IFS Briefing Note 159.

Brueckner, M. and Lederman, D. (2015) Effects of Income Inequality on Aggregate Output. Policy Research working paper no. WPS 7317. Washington, DC: World Bank Group.

Burkhauser, R., Hérault, N., Jenkins, S. and Wilkins, R. (2018a) Top Incomes and Inequality in the UK: Reconciling Estimates from Household Survey and Tax Return Data. *Oxford Economic Papers, 70:* 301–26. doi: 10.1093/oep/gpx041

Burkhauser, R., Hérault, N., Jenkins, S. and Wilkins, R. (2018b) Survey Under-Coverage of Top Incomes and Estimation of Inequality: What Is The Role of the UK's SPI Adjustment? *Fiscal Studies, 39*(2), 213–40.

Carney, M. (2014) Inclusive capitalism – creating a sense of the systemic. Speech at the Conference on Inclusive Capitalism, London, 27 May, www.bis.org/review/r140528b.htm

Chang, H. (2010) *23 Things They Don't Tell You About Capitalism.* Harmondsworth: Penguin.

Chetty, R., Grusky, D., Hell, M., Hendren, N., Manduca, R. and Narang, J. (2017) The Fading American Dream: Trends in Absolute Income Mobility Since 1940. *Science 356*(6336), 398–406.

Cingano, F. (2014) Trends in Income Inequality and its Impact on Economic Growth. *OECD* Social, Employment and Migration Working Papers, No. 163. Paris: OECD. doi: 10.1787/5jxrjncwxv6j-en

Clark, T. and Leicester, A. (2004) Inequality and Two Decades of British Tax and Benefit Reforms. *Fiscal Studies*, 25, 129–58. doi: 10.1111/j.1475-5890.2004. tb00100.x

Collinson, A. (2019) Zero-hours contracts: time to stamp them out, www.tuc.org.uk/blogs/zero-hours-contracts-time-stamp-them-out

Corak, M. (2013a) Income Inequality, Equality of Opportunity, and Intergenerational Mobility. *Journal of Economic Perspectives*, 27(3), 79–102.

Corak, M. (2013b) Inequality from Generation to Generation: The United States in Comparison. In Robert Rycroft (ed.), *The Economics of Inequality, Poverty, and Discrimination in the 21st Century*. Santa Barbara, CA: ABC-CLIO.

Corfe, S. and Keohane, N. (2018) *Measuring the Poverty Premium*. London: The Social Market Foundation.

Crawford, C., Macmillan, L. and Vignoles, A. (2017) When and Why Do Initially High-Achieving Poor Children Fall Behind? *Oxford Review of Education*, 43(1), 88–108. doi: 10.1080/03054985.2016.1240672

Crawford, R. and Hood, A. (2015) A tale of three distributions: inheritances, wealth and lifetime income, Institute for Fiscal Studies WP 15/14.

Cribb, J., Hood, A., Joyce, R. and Norris Keiller, A. (2017) *Living Standards, Poverty and Inequality in the UK: 2017*. London: Institute for Fiscal Studies.

Cribb, J., Norris Keiller, A. and Waters, T. (2018) *Living Standards, Poverty and Inequality in the UK: 2018*. London: Institute for Fiscal Studies.

Cummins, N. (2019) The missing English middle class? Evidence from 60 million death and probate records, https://voxeu.org/article/missing-english-middle-class-evidence-60-million-death-and-probate-records

Dabla-Norris, E., Kochhar, K., Suphaphiphat, N., Ricka, F. and Tsounta, E. (2015) Causes and Consequences of Income Inequality: A Global Perspective, SDN/15/13, International Monetary Fund.

D'Arcy, C. (2018) *Low Pay Britain 2018*. London: Resolution Foundation, www.resolutionfoundation.org/publications/low-pay-britain-2018/

D'Arcy, C. and Gardiner, L. (2017) *The Generation of Wealth: Asset Accumulation across and within Cohorts*. London: Resolution Foundation.

De Agostini, P., Hills, J., and Sutherland, H. (2018) Were We Really All in it Together? The Distributional Effects of the 2010–15 UK Coalition Government's Tax-benefit Policy Changes. *Social Policy & Administration*, 52, 929–49. doi: 10.1111/spol.12344.

de Botton, A. (2005) *Status Anxiety*. Harmondsworth: Penguin.

de Graaf, J., Wann, D. and Naylor, T. (2001, revised 2014) *Affluenza: The All-Consuming Epidemic*. Oakland, CA: Berrett-Koehler.

Department for Business, Energy and Industrial Strategy (2018) *The Good Work Plan* (Cm 9755). London: TSO.

Doepke, M. and Zilibotti, F. (2019) *Love, Money and Parenting: How Economics Explains The Way We Raise Our Kids*. Princeton, NJ: Princeton University Press.

Dorling, D., Stuart, B. and Stubbs, J. (2016) Brexit, inequality and the demographic divide, https://blogs.lse.ac.uk/politicsandpolicy/brexit-inequality-and-the-demographic-divide/

Dorling, D. and Thomas, B. (2016) *People and Places: A 21st-Century Atlas of the UK*. Bristol: The Policy Press.

DWP (Department for Work and Pensions) (2019) Households Below Average Income: An analysis of the UK income distribution: 1994/95-2017/18, www.gov.uk/government/statistics/households-below-average-income-199495-to-201718

Edmans, A. and Gabaix, X. (2016) Executive Compensation: A Modern Primer. *Journal of Economic Literature*, 54(4), 1232–87. doi: 10.1257/jel.20161153

Elliot Major, L. and Machin. S. (2018) *Social Mobility and its Enemies*. London: Pelican.

Förster, M., Llena-Nozal, A. and Nafilyan, V. (2014) Trends in Top Incomes and their Taxation in OECD Countries, OECD Social, Employment and Migration Working Papers, No. 159. Paris: OECD doi: 10.1787/5jz43jhlz87f-en

Francis, B. and Hutchings, M. (2013) Parent Power? Using money and information to boost children's chances of educational success. The Sutton Trust.

Friedman, S. and Laurison, D. (2019) *The Class Ceiling: Why it Pays to be Privileged*. London: Pelican.

Gardiner, L. (2017) The Million Dollar Be-Question. The Resolution Foundation.

Garnero, A., Hijzen, A. and Martin, S. (2019) More Unequal, but More Mobile? Earnings Inequality and Mobility in OECD Countries. *Labour Economics, 56*, 26–35, doi: 10.1016/j.labeco.2018.08.005

Giles, C. (2018) Britain's social ills cannot be blamed on rising inequality. *Financial Times*, 29 March.

Goulden, C. (2018) Universal Basic Income – not the answer to poverty, www.jrf.org.uk/blog/universal-basic-income-not-answer-poverty

Grigoli, F. and Nobles, A. (2017) The Inequality Overhang, International Monetary Fund Working Paper WP/17/76.

High Pay Commission (2011) Cheques with Balances: Why tackling high pay is in the national interest.

Hills, J., Bastagli, F., Cowell, F., Glennerster, H., Karagiannaki, E. and McKnight, A. (2013) *Wealth in the UK: Distribution, Accumulation, and Policy*. Oxford: Oxford University Press.

HMRC (HM Revenue and Customs) (2012) The Exchequer effect of the 50 per cent additional rate of income tax.

HMRC (HM Revenue and Customs) (2018a) Survey of Personal Incomes, 2015–2016: Public Use Tape. [data collection]. UK Data Service. SN: 8355, doi: 10.5255/UKDA-SN-8355-1

HMRC (HM Revenue and Customs) (2018b) Inheritance Tax Statistics 2015 to 2016, www.gov.uk/government/collections/inheritance-tax-statistics

HMRC (HM Revenue and Customs) (2019) Percentile points from 1 to 99 for total income before and after tax, www.gov.uk/government/statistics/percentile-points-from-1-to-99-for-total-income-before-and-after-tax

Hood, A. and Joyce, R. (2017) Inheritances and Inequality across and within Generations, Institute for Fiscal Studies BN 192.

Irwin, N. (2019) Elizabeth Warren Wants a Wealth Tax: How Would That Even Work? *New York Times*, 18 February.

James, O. (2007) *Affluenza*. London: Vermilion.

Jenkins, S. (1995) Accounting for Inequality Trends: Decomposition Analyses for the UK, 1971–86. *Economica*, 62, 29–63.

Jenkins, S. (2011) *Changing Fortunes: Income Mobility and Poverty Dynamics in Britain*. Oxford: Oxford University Press.

Jerrim, J. and Macmillan, L. (2015) Income Inequality, Intergenerational Mobility, and the Great Gatsby Curve: Is Education the Key? *Social Forces*, 94(2), 505–53. doi: 10.1093/sf/sov075

Jones, O. (2014) *The Establishment*. Harmondsworth: Penguin.

Keeley, B. (2015) *Income Inequality: The Gap Between Rich and Poor*, OECD Insights, Paris. doi: 10.1787/9789264246010-en

Krueger, A. (2012) The Rise and Consequences of Inequality in the United States. Remarks as Prepared for Delivery for Speech at the Center for American Progress, 12 January.

Kumhof, M., Rancière, R. and Winant, P. (2015) Inequality, Leverage, and Crises. *American Economic Review*, 105(3), 1217–45. doi: 10.1257/aer.20110683

Lindley, J. and Machin, S. (2013) Wage Inequality in the Labour Years. *Oxford Review of Economic Policy*, 29(1), 167–77.

Machin, S. (2011) Changes in UK Wage Inequality over the Last Forty Years. In P. Gregg and J. Wadsworth (eds), *The Labour Market in Winter: The State of Working Britain*. Oxford: Oxford University Press. doi: 10.1093/acprof:os obl/9780199587377.001.0001

Madsen, J. (2017) Is Inequality Increasing in r-g? Piketty's Principle of Capitalist Economics and the Dynamics of Inequality in Britain, 1210-2013, CAMA Working Paper 63/2017, Crawford School of Public Policy, Australia National University.

Madsen, J. (2019) Wealth and Inequality over Eight Centuries of British Capitalism. *Journal of Development Economics*, doi: 10.1016/j.deveco.2019.01.005

Madsen, J., Rabiul Islam, Md. and Doucouliagos, H. (2018) Inequality, Financial Development and Economic Growth in the OECD, 1870–2011. *European Economic Review*, 101, 605–24.

Marmot, M. (2004) *Status Syndrome*. London: Bloomsbury.

Mijs, J. (2019) The Paradox of Inequality: Income Inequality and Belief in Meritocracy Go Hand in Hand. *Socio-Economic Review*, doi: 10.1093/ser/mwy051

Milburn, A. (2017) The government is unable to commit to the social mobility challenge. *Guardian*, 2 December.

Mirrlees, J., Adam, S., Besley, T., Blundell, R., Bond, S., Chote, R., Gammie, M., Johnson, P., Myles, G. and Poterba, J. (2011) *The Mirrlees Review*. Oxford: Oxford University Press.

Norris Keiller, A. and Waters, T. (2018) Distributional Analysis, IFS, www.ifs.org.uk/uploads/budgets/budget2018/ank_budget2018.pdf

OECD (Organization for Economic Cooperation and Development) (n.d.) What Are Equivalence Scales? www.oecd.org/els/soc/OECD-Note-Equivalence Scales.pdf

OECD (Organization for Economic Cooperation and Development) (2019) Trade Unions: Trade union density. OECD Employment and Labour Market Statistics (database), 9 March, doi: 10.1787/data-00371-en

OBR (Office for Budget Responsibility) (2019) Economic and fiscal outlook, March 2019 (CP 50). London: The Stationery Office.

ONS (Office for National Statistics) (2018a) Wealth in Great Britain Wave 5: 2014 to 2016: Corrected version 18 March 2019, www.ons.gov.uk/peoplepopulationandcommunity/personalandhouseholdfinances/incomeandwealth/bulletins/wealthingreatbritainwave5/2014to2016

ONS (Office for National Statistics) (2018b) Intergenerational transfers: the distribution of inheritances, gifts and loans, Great Britain: 2014 to 2016, www.ons.gov.uk/peoplepopulationandcommunity/personalandhouseholdfinances/incomeandwealth/articles/intergenerationaltransfersthedistributionofinheritancesgiftsandloans/2018-10-30

ONS (Office for National Statistics) (2019a) UK labour market: February 2019, www.ons.gov.uk/employmentandlabourmarket/peopleinwork/employmentandemployeetypes/bulletins/uklabourmarket/february2019#average-weekly-earnings

ONS (Office for National Statistics) (2019b) The effects of taxes and benefits on household income, disposable income estimate: 2018, wwwons.gov.uk/peoplepopulationandcommunity/personalandhouseholdfinances/incomeandwealth/datasets/householddisposableincomeandinequality

ONS (Office for National Statistics) (2019c) Using tax data to better capture top earners in household income inequality statistics, www.ons.gov.uk/peoplepopulationandcommunity/personalandhouseholdfinances/incomeandwealth/articles/usingtaxdatatobettercapturetopearnersinhouseholdincomeinequalitystatistics/2019-02-26

Ostry, J., Berg, A. and Tsangarides, C. (2014) Redistribution, Inequality and Growth, SDN/14/02, International Monetary Fund.

Ostry, J., Loungani, P. and Berg, A. (2019) *Confronting Inequality: How Societies Can Choose Inclusive Growth*. New York: Columbia University Press.

Piketty, T. (2014) *Capital in the Twenty-First Century*. Cambridge, MA: Harvard University Press.

Piketty, T., Saez, E. and Stantcheva, S. (2014) Optimal Taxation of Top Labor Incomes: A Tale of Three Elasticities. *American Economic Journal: Economic Policy*, 6(1), 230–71.

Piketty, T., Saez, E. and Zucman, G. (2018) Distributional National Accounts: Methods and Estimates for the United States. *Quarterly Journal of Economics*, 133(2), 553–609.

Piketty Symposium (2014) *British Journal of Sociology*, *65*, 589–90. doi: 10.1111/ 1468-4446.12113

Plunkett, J. and Hurrell, A. (2013) Fifteen years later: A discussion paper on the future of the UK National Minimum Wage and Low Pay Commission, The Resolution Foundation.

Pooley, C. R. (2019) Top UK CEOs earn annual wage of average worker in 2½ days. *Financial Times*, 4 January.

Ray, D. (2015) Nit-Piketty: A Comment on Thomas Piketty's *Capital in the Twenty First Century*. *CESifo Forum*, *16*(1), 19–25.

Reed, H. (2014) Piketty, Chris Giles and wealth inequality: it's all about the discontinuities. *Guardian*, 29 May.

Resolution Foundation (2019) Super, Smashing, Great? Spring Statement response March 2019, www.resolutionfoundation.org/publications/super-smashing-great-spring-statement-2019-response/

Robeyns, I. (2016) Having Too Much. In J. Knight and M. Schwarzberg (eds), *Wealth: NOMOS LVI*. New York: New York University Press.

Robinson, N. (2019) Alexandria Ocasio-Cortez is right. A 70% tax on the rich makes sense. *Guardian*, 8 January.

Roemer, J. and Trannoy, A. (2016) Equality of Opportunity: Theory and Measurement. *Journal of Economic Literature*, *54*(4), 1288–332. doi: 10.1257/ jel.20151206

Rowlingson, K. (2011) *Does Income Inequality Cause Health and Social Problems?* York: The Joseph Rowntree Foundation.

Rubolino, E. and Waldenström, D. (2017a) Tax Progressivity and Top Incomes: Evidence from Tax Reforms. *IZA Discussion Paper 10666*.

Rubolino, E. and Waldenström, D. (2017b) Trends and Gradients in Top Tax Elasticities: Cross-Country Evidence, 1900–2014. IZA Discussion Paper 10667.

Savage, M. (2015) *Social Class in the 21st Century*. London: Pelican.

Simms, M. (2019) *What Do We Know and What Should We Do About the Future of Work?* London: Sage.

Smith, M., Yagan, D., Zidar, O. and Zwick, E. (2019) Capitalists in the Twenty-First Century, NBER WP 25442.

Stiglitz, J. E. (2012) *The Price of Inequality*. Harmondsworth: Penguin.

Stiglitz, J.E. (2015) Inequality and Economic Growth. *Political Quarterly*, *86*, 134–55. doi: 10.1111/1467-923X.12237

Sutton Trust (2017) Mobility Manifesto 2017, www.suttontrust.com/wp-content/ uploads/2017/07/Mobility-Manifesto-2017_FINAL.pdf

Tanndal, J. and Waldenström, D. (2018) Does Financial Deregulation Boost Top Incomes? Evidence from the Big Bang. *Economica*, *85*, 232–65. doi: 10.1111/ ecca.12247

The Intergenerational Commission (2018) *A New Generational Contract*. London: Resolution Foundation.

United Nations (2009) Report of the Commission of Experts of the President of the United Nations General Assembly on Reforms of the International Monetary and Financial System, New York.

Veblen, T. (1899) *The Theory of the Leisure Class: An Economic Study in the Evolution of Institutions*. New York: Macmillan.

Wealth and Inequality (2015) *Journal of Economic Perspectives, 29*(1), 3–88.

Wilkinson, R. and Pickett, K. (2009) *The Spirit Level*. Harmondsworth: Penguin.

Wilkinson, R. and Pickett, K. (2018) *The Inner Level*. London: Penguin Random House.

Willetts, D. (2010) *The Pinch*. London: Atlantic Books.

Young, C. (2017) *The Myth of Millionaire Tax Flight: How Place Still Matters For The Rich*. Stanford, CA: Stanford University Press.

Young, C., Varner, C., Lurie, I. Z. and Prisinzano, R. (2016) Millionaire Migration and Taxation of the Elite: Evidence from Administrative Data. *American Sociological Review, 81*(3), 421–46. doi: 10.1177/0003122416639625

Zucman, G. (2019) Global Wealth Inequality, NBER WP 25462.

index